BOOK VII

DECODING
THE SACRED ALPHABET AND NUMEROLOGY
METAPHYSICAL INTERPRETATION

O.M. KELLY

COPYRIGHT

Copyright © 2023 Margret Ann Kelly/O.M. Kelly
Series: Book VII Republished
First Published as Book VII in "Decoding the Mind of God",
Margret Ann Kelly/O.M. Kelly, Copyright © 2011.
ISBN: 978-0-6458487-5-5

All rights reserved. This book may not be reproduced, wholly or in part, or transmitted in any form whatsoever without written permission from the author, O.M. Kelly, www.elanea.com.

The author of this book does not dispense medical advice or prescribe the use of any technique as a form of treatment for physical, emotional, or medical problems without the advice of a physician, either directly or indirectly. The intent of the author is only to offer information of a general nature to help you in your quest for emotional and spiritual well-being. In the event you use any of the information in this book for yourself, which is your constitutional right, the author assumes no responsibility for your actions.

AUTHOR

Author O. M. Kelly, known as Omni to her clients and students is an accomplished author and international lecturer, on Metaphysics, Philosophy and understanding the Collective Consciousness. Omni consults for Member States of the European Commission as a Conciliation Advisor and Rhetoric Counsellor for other International Companies throughout Europe. Omni now resides on Australia's beautiful Gold Coast, writing books, and works as a Life Mentor and Business Coach.

Omni has dedicated her life to decoding the mysteries of the universe. With a deep knowledge of the biblical agenda, mythologies including ancient Egyptology, Asian principles, and metaphysical insights, Omni has discovered the secret that all stories share a coded hidden metaphysical language. Her seminal work, "Decoding the Mind of God", is a compilation of nine volumes of metaphysical information based on the research into the coded information of the Laws of the Universe, also known as the Collective Consciousness, and represents a groundbreaking contribution to our understanding of the metaphysical universe. Now, all nine volumes are being released as separate, revised books, each offering a unique perspective on the universe's workings. Omni's work has been widely acclaimed for its depth of insight, and her contributions to the field of metaphysics have been groundbreaking.

THIS BOOK

Prepare for a mind-expanding journey! "Decoding The Sacred Alphabet & Numerology" is not just a book – it's an invitation to explore an unparalleled perspective on the Metaphysical realm of language and numbers. Omni's revelations will not only deepen your grasp of ancient Metaphysical sacred codes but also shed light on the profound influence of names and numbers, including your very own.

Dive into a world of Metaphysical knowledge as this captivating book unravels the intricate connections between higher consciousness, names, places, and numbers. Omni, with a deep knowledge into biblical agendas, mythologies, Egyptology, Asian principles, and metaphysical insights, has cracked the code of the hidden metaphysical language. Unveil the extraordinary realm of Metaphysical Numerology, where numbers reveal personality traits and life paths. Omni guides you through the intricate process, offering a roadmap to spiritual insight and a clearer understanding of your life's purpose.

Imagine deciphering the hidden messages that surround you daily! As you master the Metaphysical Sacred Alphabet and Numerology codes, new horizons of awareness will expand before you. Embark on a voyage through time and myth, from the enigmas of Babylon and Shambhala to the wonders of Luxor, Giza, and beyond. Traverse the mystical journey of Solomon's Temple and uncover the timeless secrets of Akhenaton and Tomb KV-63. Venture deep into Grecian tales, decoded through the metaphysical language, and traverse the historic Old Silk Road like never before.

Are you ready to embrace a journey of self-discovery? Join O.M. Kelly in an expedition to uncover the divine language woven into the fabric of our existence. "Decoding The Sacred Alphabet & Numerology" is more than a book – it's a transformative experience waiting to be explored. Embrace the power of ancient wisdom.

CONTENT

Introduction

Chapter One
The Sacred Alphabet — Page 1

Chapter Two
Your Name — Page 5

Chapter Three
The Alphabetic Inheritance Of Babylon — Page 13

Chapter Four
Ages Of The Collective Soul — Page 18

Chapter Five
The Language Of The Divine Inheritance — Page 21

Chapter Six
The Journey Of The Myth — Page 24

Chapter Seven
Babylon And Shambhala — Page 28

Chapter Eight
The Sacred Language — Page 31

Chapter Nine
The Language Of The Divine Babylon — Page 35

Chapter Ten
The Universal Language Is You Discovering Your Temple Of Light — Page 38

Chapter Eleven
The White And Blue Nile — Page 42

Chapter Twelve
Luxor – Where The Intellectual Light Of The Oracle Releases — Page 46

Chapter Thirteen
The Delta — Page 51

Chapter Fourteen
Giza, Saqqara, And Faiyum — Page 55

Chapter Fifteen
Solomon's Temple — Page 59

Chapter Sixteen
The Sacred Journey Into The Unconscious Realms   Page 66

Chapter Seventeen
Akhenaton   Page 69

Chapter Eighteen
Tomb KV-63   Page 71

Chapter Nineteen
How We Unweave The Threads Of Our DNA   Page 76

Chapter Twenty
The Old Aramaic Story Of Aladdin And The Lamp   Page 78

Chapter Twenty One
Grecian Stories Through The Metaphysical
Language   Page 80

Chapter Twenty Two
Travelling Along the Old Silk Road   Page 87

Chapter Twenty Three
Electromagnetic Energy Fields Coincide
Throughout The Universes   Page 90

Chapter Twenty Four
My Journey   Page 91

Chapter Twenty Five
Returning Home To Babylon   Page 94

Chapter Twenty Six
Numerology   Page 96

Chapter Twenty Seven
The Shamanic Inheritance Of Numbers And
Their Meanings   Page 104

Chapter Twenty Eight
How We Rely On Numbers To Read The Hidden
Language   Page 108

Chapter Twenty Nine
The Divine Language   Page 113

Books By O.M. Kelly (Omni)   Page 125

INTRODUCTION

In writing the book of the Sacred Alphabet and Numerology, I became fascinated with the explanation to how we first began to tune in to the mathematics of the Collective Consciousness. We began to acknowledge first ourselves, and then others, through our feelings creating our inner sounds. Where did these sounds come from? How did we learn to hear, accept, and then speak them? The research into these teachings continued for many years of my life. The language of the planet has been broken up as our emotional intelligence urged us forward, and it became the language of "Bja-Ab-EL-On" (Babylon).

Through the passing of time, we began to intellectually gather together our verse, and we grew into a conversation with one another. The small collective of the tribe we belonged to was forming its own language. I am coming to the conclusion that "Bab-EL-on" and "Bib-EL-on" have the same meaning. It is just that one became more advanced than the other, where our attitude was transformed into becoming our intelligence. Our inner Bible began to communicate when our mind was at rest – where we are free to slip in and out of our parallel worlds with ease, as we learn to see how our personalities are releasing to one another to become our inner strength.

We read of old stories from all cultures – whether it be Aboriginal, Mayan, Asian, Mesopotamian, etc. – and, from these parallels, we have the opportunity to use these stories and sounds to our benefit. When we hear a word, its sound vibrates throughout the mathematics of our DNA. All is registered with the inner library of the mind. Each word awaits us, and is in reference to us, as we create a sentence to speak.

This book has so much information; please read it slowly to absorb that information correctly. Some of my students have had to read the words many times over, and, each time they reread the words, they lifted another layer and earned something new.

CHAPTER ONE

The Sacred Alphabet

The alphabet began when man first learned to communicate and express his desires – that is, explain his inner self to someone else. The grunt came first, as a result of the evolution of man's sexual energy, which is the first step to the awakening of the mind. One of the first sounds we uttered was "ng", as this was how our muscles had to prepare themselves to release and surge our sound forward; from that exercise, man learned to open his mouth in order to allow the creation of other sounds. In the beginning, the most commonly used letters were n and m, as these two letters came from deep within, where each human felt comfortable in expressing the sounds that these two letters represented. Other sounds and letters were added as we evolved, with the last two being the letters j and u. Over time, the inner alphabet has changed – we have added to it and rearranged it, through opening up and broadening our intelligence in order to hear ourselves releasing our thoughts and feelings.

When they speak in their native languages, the Australian Aborigines still use the "ng" sound at the beginning of many of their words. They say "ngelea" as a greeting of welcome. If we take this word back through the sacred codes of the DNA of human evolution, "ng-EL-EA" is the pronunciation of the names of the first God "EL" and the third God "EA", with the primordial "ng" at the beginning.

Through the salutation that the Aborigines have presented to us through their language, the word is in relationship to us earning our way up through the pathways of the inner Gods, in order for them to come together to become one God. We begin to acknowledge our own heavenly kingdom when we desire a word to release on behalf of what we feel we want to say. So the word "ngelea" denotes that they are welcoming the whole person, from their toes right up through to their crown.

When we go back to the first language of man, we can see

the evolution of the Sacred Alphabet, as well as how the collection of our tribal heritage has programmed our own language into us, which autonomically creates our own intelligence. Our language – or "land-gauge" is where we learn to mathematically gauge or measure the intelligence of ourselves in order to feel comfortable releasing it out to the rest of humanity.

The following text that is explained in this book may sound complicated if you are a beginner; it was that way for me, too. I had to persevere for many strenuous years to bring it all together in order to finally accomplish this wonderful history of our past. Please read it in a conservative manner, through the respect that you are responsible for returning to your ancestors; you are now acknowledging and returning the Collective Inheritance that your cells have busily collected over thousands of years to create your family tribe. I have danced my way around the planet many times, explaining this story to many different languages; each time, I am able to release and speak more of my Collective Inheritance as the codes are released through the freedom that I have earned and felt within myself.

From the moment of your gestation, your memory banks become embedded with this information; this is a repertoire presented to you through the Divine Inheritance to explain to you why and how your Soul was designed to be here – why you were placed here as a quasar to represent your family. This was all happened nine months before you inhaled your first breath of air. All this intellectuality springs forth through you religiously asking yourself a question – which is created through an emotional response to those memories, and which allows them to release into the personalities that create your thinking. Read the text over again until you feel comfortable; only then will you know that you have reminded yourself of the connection that you have made with those ancient memories that have created your past. These are the pages of the second God "AN"; they are the books of your inner library – the recorded history of your grandmothers and grandfathers and of all your ancestors. I will initiate you into some of the basic structure of words that we use to urge ourselves forward. We can add to, but not subtract from, this list of words. This list will allow you to learn the codes of the Sacred Alphabet, which you will repeat according to your own intelligence accepting the nurturing from its self. Through your belief in your self, and through your accepting your intellectual advantages for your own personal gain, you will see these words change.

The Basic Codes to the Sacred Alphabet

A.　　Ascension. Activate. Attitude. Antenna.

B.　　Before. Beginning. Balance. Beauty.

C.　　Creation. Christ. Create. Comply. Complete.

D.　　Depth. Death. Desire. Define. Divine. Divinity.

E.　　Energy. Eternal. Evolve. Essence.

F.　　Fate. Faith. Form. Freedom. Fly.

G.　　God. Greatness. Gift.

H.　　Have. Hold. Horizon. Highness. Heaven.

I.　　Intelligence. Intuition.

J.　　Jesus. Judgment. Justice.

K.　　Knowledge. Knowing. Knife.

L.　　Love. Light. Life.

M.　　Measure. Master. Martyr.

N.　　Nourish. Nurture.

O.　　Oracle. Oneness.

P.　　Power. Pulse. Presence. Potent.

Q.　　Quest. Question. Query. Queen. Quell. Quintessence.

R. Release. Reign. Royal.

S. Search. Soul. Spirit. Sword. Source. Sound.

T. Trial. Trust. Truth. Tone.

U. Understanding. Urge. Uphold. Upon. Unto.

V. Victory. Valour. Value.

W. Wise. Wisdom. Will. Wind. Weave.

X. Xenium. (Latin: "to see the measurement from within")

Y. Yearn. Young. Yield. Yoke.

Z. Zenith.

Notes:

CHAPTER TWO

Your Name

You were given a name at birth (in the Western world, this is called our "Christian name"), and that name is a coded recollection of the challenges that you have the possibilities to live, through your own achievements. Some of us respect the name we are called; others of us dislike our name; most of us just accept the fact that our names are of no consequence. That is wrong! Through the Sacred Alphabet, your name belongs to one of your tribes – your name calls you to live your tribal sound, pulse, and tone. That sound has a life force which connects you to the blueprint of the Collective Consciousness; it is always there to support and answer to you. Your pulse releases the mathematics of the name you are called. And the tone places you into the right place, where you inherit your own DNA. The name you were given at birth is no mistake! You are the Genes of Isis – or the Book of Genesis – for, they are one and the same.

Some sons are named after their father or grandfather, and that process is used respectfully to remember that member of the family. On the other hand, maybe we, as parents, just had a great liking for that person and wanted to mirror his name onto our son. I did that with one of my sons. This automatically grids the child back into that vibration, and so he will also take on the consequences of that inheritance. Every thought of familiar inheritance is stored in your memory banks. Think clearly about the name you give your child! The mathematical light that shines through his/her given name must be understood, and accounted for, by the child.

When someone joins the army in Australia, he usually begins as a lance corporal, who represents the mind of oneself, and he is initiated into becoming a soldier in training; if he obeys the rules and proves himself worthy, he will be promoted to corporal. The "lance" represents the piercing of the mind. The army represents the government of the land, and it sets a standard that each person who joins must bear. Everyone who joins must obey this set of rules; as he advances his education within this set of rules, his title changes, which promotes him up the ladder and gives him greater responsibilities to uphold.

The Spiritual journey is exactly the same. As we evolve from the third dimension into the fourth, our acceptance of self has to take on an added responsibility, and so we are often presented with another name. In some religions, those who have professed their faith, must also release the name from their old life and take on a new name of a sacred reference to the standard they must bear.

My name has changed along the way, but the difference for me was that my journey was to understand the codes to the language of the Hidden God. The Sacred Alphabet is inscribed in the Collective Consciousness, as are the Laws of the Universe, which state that, when one steps up into the firmament, these laws must be obeyed. Through the commitment that one makes, no half-hearted measures or excuses are allowed or accepted. There were many names that I have had to birth myself through in order to understand the changes of the levels of intellectual mathematics that were being presented to me. Everyone who has accepted his/her next evolutionary quest goes through the same process. We may have that new name for months or years, depending on our own evolutionary process; and, once we have earned its level of conduct, the code of our forthcoming inheritance is presented to us – always with an added responsibility, so that we may exalt ourselves again.

Write your given name on a piece of paper, and then look up what it means using the list in the "Basic Codes to the Sacred Alphabet" in the previous chapter. Place the words into a sentence to see the story of what you have the opportunity to achieve and accomplish. (Use the "Examples of Decoded Names" below to assist you.) Study this, looking at yourself truthfully, and then ask yourself what you have to change within so that you can evolve that name into a much higher vibration. By accepting this added responsibility, you will receive the keys to unlock your own inner wisdom – which will introduce you into your DNA – so that you can evolve your life, and allow it to become much easier for you to live and understand.

Examples of Decoded Names

Remember, first we use the codes from the list, and then we create a sentence using those words.

FELICITY: Feeling – Energy – Life – Intellect – Creates – Intelligence – Truth – Yearning. Through Feeling my Energy, my Life has matured, my Intellect Creates my Intelligence and releases my Truth through my Yearning to understand myself.

ULRIKE: Understanding – Life – Release – Intelligence Knowledge – Evermore. Through Understanding my Life, I Release my Intelligence and Knowledge for Evermore.

BEATRICE: Balancing – Eternal – Attitude – Truth – Releases – Intelligence – Consciousness – Evermore. Through Balancing my Eternal Attitude, my Truth Releases my Intelligence throughout the Consciousness Evermore.

LUNA: Life – Understanding – Nourish – Ascend. Through my Life's Understanding, I Nourish as I Ascend.

SANDRA: Soul – Action – Nourished – Divine – Releasing – Ascension. Through my Souls Action, I am Nourished through the Divine Releasing my Ascension.

NAOMI: Nourish – Ascend – Oracle – Master – Intelligence. Through Nourishing, I will Ascend the Oracle and Master my Intelligence.

PETER: Power – Eternal – Truth – Evolve – Release. Through the Power of Eternal Truth, I Evolve and Release.

ANNA: Ascend and Nurture, Nurture and Ascend. (It is difficult to design a clear sentence for this one! This poor girl has to keep on looking at her own reflection. Anna is the angel; she does not want to put her feet on the ground. Anna knows it all but has great difficulty in learning how to put that knowledge out there. Look at your friends or family who have the name Anna and see how many emotional excuses they make in order to satisfy themselves and others.)

MARGRET: Master – Ascend – Release – God – Release – Eternal – Truth. Mastering and Ascending to Release God through releasing Eternal Truth. Margret is my given name, and that is the spelling my parents chose – there is no a after the g, as in the more common version of Margaret. In Aramaic, the name means "the gate, the arch, or the ark". By opening the gate, we open the door of the temple. We have come from out of the wild up to the door, and we pass through an archway, which represents the church – or the energy of the DNA – releasing itself through to the next level. Some people are given three or four names at birth, so their parents are trying to show them that they have many opportunities to release the bondage of their DNA. By giving their children many names, parents give them the energy of the alphabet to help them through.

Question: I have three given names: Judith Helena Elizabeth. Can you tell me what they mean?

Answer: Judith is a very powerful name; you must speak your truth and also live by the Divine Law. People with the name Judith are usually very strict in their religious way of life. Helena is always at war within herself; she is always arguing and will not give up. Elizabeth has the nature of the dragon, and so she says, "I will do nothing!" Look to your mother to see why she gave you that name. Poor Elizabeth must always use her left brain! She says, "Emotions? I have no time for emotions. I do not have the time to feel."

Every Elizabeth who comes to me has brilliant ideas but great difficulty putting them in motion. Elizabeth also has an immense amount of intelligence. Look at other people in your life with the name Elizabeth, and you will see how their ego steps in all the time to stop them from inheriting themselves. Your personalities have to stand to attention and change as someone calls your name; this also happens as you speak your name to someone else.

Were you ever given a nickname as a child? That name came from someone close to you who noticed another vibration of intelligence included in your thinking, so they changed your name to suit their compatibility regarding you on their inner level. Someone saw the light in you that others did not. A nickname "nicks" or cuts our name. (Was that the challenge of the one called Enoch? Or, if we look at this name through the ancient language, it is pronounced "Eunuch", who was castrated; or, when this is understood correctly, whose "cast was rated by God". Wow! That deserves some thought!) Remember the name of Santa Claus; his name in most lands who still speak their old language is Saint Nicklaus. Sometimes, the more familiar we become with someone, the more we abbreviate their name. For example, Margret becomes Meg; Patricia becomes Pat; William becomes Bill; Robert becomes Bob; John becomes Jack; James becomes Jim; Joseph becomes Joe; and so on. When we abbreviate someone's name, it means that he/she has just about outgrown it and is ready to evolve into the next one.

Your given name is also the opposite of how you genetically think and what you want to believe in; in this way, it reveals what you must become in order to fulfil your inheritance. Through the mind of your parents, you were given a name, and you took on that responsibility on their behalf. You had to become both the satisfaction of their ego and the balance of their emotions. As parents, some of you have difficulties in giving your child the right name. On a subconscious level, you are giving your child your own expectations of what you yourself wish to become, not necessarily what you are expecting your child to become, but be aware that you are giving your child this responsibility through the name that you choose.

Your family name – or surname – is your tribal name; it is the results of your DNA. In many old cultures, your tribal name is said first (this is the case throughout most of the East). This was how the Aborigines accepted me; I was not referred to as Mrs Kelly, I was referred to as Kelly Mrs. Through the old ways, my past inheritance was respected through their heart and returned to me.

Your birth name is a vibration of sound that you hear on an unconscious level, which is then notified and registered throughout every one of your cells. The name is heard, and then it collects through your cells, travelling throughout the body, up into the unconscious mind, and into the Collective Consciousness and Inheritance. (You will notice that teenage boys refer and call out to their friends by their tribal names. This is an ancient calling that they have released as they grow into their warrior in order to initiate their own wisdom.)

When the sound of your name is finally accepted and has seated itself in your Soul, the brain takes over, and you have a name. If you cannot accept your name, the best way you can help yourself is to say the vibration of that name backwards, and you will then find the missing link – that missing link is the weakness in your mind that prevents you from accepting your self in the moment.

When we say our name forward, it supports our ego; through saying our name backwards, it reflects through to your emotions. Write your name down backwards. Decode it using the Sacred Alphabet, and you will see yourself through different eyes. Say your name backwards to help you understand who you really are – it makes you become much more aware of this title that you have been born into; by using this method, your reversed name becomes a mirror image of you, which changes your attitude on an emotional level.

By creating this experience you are changing your reflection, which alerts the mathematics of your mind to experience the feelings that collect in your right brain, but not necessarily in your left. My seminar students have enjoyed many hours of laughter during this explanation, as they woke up to their own excuses in regard to how they have overprotected themselves through not truthfully accepting their given names.

Through the Sacred Alphabet, each letter is created through the Soul energy releasing its own movement. Metaphysically and mythically, we have named this the Holy Grail. This cooperation of letters works up into the unconscious mind, as it is produced from the way you hear the sound of your name. When the unconscious mind registers the sound of each syllable, it sets the scene in motion; which means that the mathematics of the mind has already set the rules that your inner library must abide by. That motion then moves through the nervous system into the glands, which, in turn, send each message through to the brain. This is where the sonic sound registers again with the lymphatic system – or web. Remember that we have three membranes that cover the brain and spinal cord: the first layer is the pia mater, which equates to the piousness of self; the second layer is the arachnoids which is alerted to every vibration that is stimulated in our aura and is where we can weave and collect ourselves together; the third and final layer is the dura mater, and this is attained through our attitude, which collects through the durability that we create through our own belief – all of which creates our spoken language.

We have given ourselves a religious experience to equate each thought up into the unconscious mind. A religious experience is when you respect yourself through your own silence. That silence awakens and opens the ventricles of your heart, and your feelings begin to spiral and create subsonic vibrations, which are measured through the Collective Inheritance of self; this distinguishes the atonement ("at-one-ment") between you and the highest form of your God within. It is also one of the first lessons in the understanding of that wonderful word that we all seem to want to use: love!

The bat (or the sphenoid bone, as mentioned in my book "Decoding Thought"), works through the sonar of sound, which ascends outwards into your auric fields, and, once it reaches its own boundary – which all depends on your intellect – it bounces back to create the movement of sonic sound. It is the essence from this movement that accumulates through the multiplication of the waves reflecting back into your body. These sublime vibrations have the responsibility of producing our communication, and, when they become harmonized, they are autonomically enhanced up into our ethereal layers, which produce our own electromagnetic fields.

When new students introduce themselves to me, I listen to their names, but I usually do not hear the names; instead, I see a higher reference of their codes through them each reaching a pinnacle in their life – that is, through them finding the strength where they allow themselves to participate in this new commitment to their inner education. Also, I sense their vibrations as to what they are expecting to interest them in their forthcoming intelligence. By the time they come to me for teaching, they have intellectually outgrown their old name (i.e., the name their parents gave them at birth). Through the new name that I am given, through my guardians to exalt the student's intellect when the student is ready, I explain the codes associated with this name and pass it on to the student. Students begin their training into their seminary steps of education, in which their Higher Self will place new challenges before them. Always remember, your next step awaits your appropriate earnings.

Notes:

CHAPTER THREE

The Alphabetic Inheritance Of Babylon

Throughout my education, I received many names; by this, I mean that I received the vibration of the name. The last vibration I received came to me in the year 2000, and I use a shortened version of it: Omni. I have had to learn and accept the language of the alphabetical inheritance to the codes of each name. For twelve years, I was known as Om Mira, and I had grown quite satisfied with that name; but, once I had conquered it, I had to release it. Both names were "nicked" in order for my students to be able to pronounce them. The reason for this new name became known to me when I went to Europe in the late '90s, as that is when I was asked to teach and explain my academic stature.

Years previously at the beginning of my education, my name changed every few days; at first, I thought it was a joke being played out on me. Slowly, I began to notice that the names were becoming stronger, longer and more difficult for me to pronounce. I realized that I was being introduced into the alphabetical inheritance of Babylon; this is explained in chapter 5 of the Book of Genesis, which describes the generations of Adam, who lived for 930 years. The biblical stories of the twelve tribes of Israel also explain the change of names (i.e., who begat whom, etc.). Thus, I realized that the names I was given in the beginning were references to the names of our own educational systems that are embedded in our DNA; these names were a challenge, designed for me to try to understand all this knowledge – and many a laugh resulted as I opened up my inner dictionary.

That was when I began to realize that I was bringing myself up and through the alignments that society takes for granted. In other words, I realized that the joke was on me – I had to answer the challenge and speak from the wisdom of the name that I had been given. My memorial genetics were opening up, and I learned to conquer those earnings in double quick time. I had to be able to master those ideologies in a matter of days; but, once I understood the title – or name – I became all of it, and my commitment to the name and the challenge became much easier.

After that point, my name was challenged and changed again; the education for that next title began as soon as I had completed the understanding of the previous one. I was working my way up through the levels of accepting the language of the unconscious mind; therefore, my earnings accelerated as my thinking became faster, and, so too, did my time. It took years of this training – through frustration beyond comprehension – for me to keep on correcting my intelligence, as I had to accept what was placed in front of me. There was no walking away from any of it; and, if I did walk away, nothing happened – my mind went into an abeyance until I could go back over my teachings and pick up from where I had left off.

So, as the names changed I realized that they were being given to me in three different levels. The beginning of the education brought forth more information from my endocrine system; this system begins to open up in our childhood, so the message was delivered to me more as a nursery rhyme, or a fairy story. As the name grew into the next level, it opened up to strengthen my immune system; this system begins to collect when we birth into our teenage years, awakening the inner warrior. Our personalities begin to unravel at that point, and our inner dictionary becomes much more colloquial; we learn to find the strength to place our own point of view out to others. As I accepted more responsibility for this education, my original name grew and became more advanced, which placed the responsibility onto my lymphatic system. The lymph we refer to as the "umbrella of God", as it weaves its way throughout the whole body; finally the adult in me had become alive. Those three stages of names brought that frequency into a dependable explanation of how I would be able to mirror myself back to humanity. The circle of energy had been completed; thus, my next world could begin. This is exactly what I explain regarding the concordance of why our stories are carved on the walls of Egypt. The wonderful ancient Egyptians have left us the initiations to succeed; they inscribed the sacred codes into the walls, as to how we can understand our journey into the afterlife – or the next world.

No, we have not gotten that story exactly right – not just yet, anyway.

Each of my Shamanic names provided a language of separation and advancement for me to grow through. As each step of my intellect unfolded, it became easier for me to find the answers to my own questions, as well as to answer those questions that I had received from others. When we accept each level of our truth, we are welcomed into a more advanced tribe in order to experience our life through these higher levels of understanding. Once I had brought all those vibrations into their fullness, through mastering myself, my life was held in abeyance until the next name came through. As I said, it took an immense amount of study over the years to earn the full Sacred Alphabet, complete with the learning capacity for each of my names. It was when I understood the language that the Bible was written in – in all its totality – that the names were transferred into me. I was pleased with my endowment of Omni, and I realized that now I must live up to it – that was my challenge and my responsibility. This placed a totally different slant on things. My total responsibility is now focused on the words that I speak, and, always, I know that my truth reigns supreme.

The vibration of the full name I received in 2000 is "Om-ni-aar-elle" (abbreviated "Omni", as I mentioned). As this name began to enter into my life, I did not want to accept the changes, at first; I felt very comfortable with my name at that time ("Om Mira"), which had supported me well. Again, as mentioned, I had been invited to Europe to teach, and I was very quickly becoming internationally renowned, speaking to many people from different lands, through many interpreters. I had moved out from the safety net of my own land, and I had not fully realized the responsibility that was being placed on my shoulders.

I refused the name Omniaarelle for six long weeks, as it seemed too hard to pronounce and far too long, but I soon learned. The number of students attending my classes was cut in half, my car broke down, my radiator burst, my phone was disconnected, and the heating system in my apartment blew up. Many cataclysmic events occurred in my life through my refusal to accept that new name. Everything stopped through my refusing to take my next breath and hold myself in abeyance; in other words, I had turned my back on myself.

The Universe would not accept excuses from me! The Cosmic Attitude is: "This is it – take it or leave it!" The prophet could not profit, so life became extremely hard, financially. I realized that the creator had stood by me through all those years of my training, and I also knew that I had to accept that this higher education I had received was not only for me, it was also for me to release this information so that all humanity could accept and understand. They would receive those understandings through the same opportunities that I had been given, and they would bring that written information back within to connect to themselves. I had worried what the new students would think when I introduced myself to them the following month; as they were just getting used to my name (Om Mira). I forgot, of course, that my ego could no longer be in control of my destiny.

I was at a turning point in my life – which happens to all of us twice a year – I had to retrace my own constituency and come back into my own palace of worthiness. The creation of all had tenderly shown me what I was here to do, which was to lead humanity into its next step of evolution of awareness. He loved me, even when my strength was at its weakest point, and he was prepared to wait until I could find myself again. As I gathered myself together, sending my love and courage back into myself, and my strength returned to support me once more. That name, which I shortened to Omni, is a code of recognition through the Collective Consciousness. Once I accepted the responsibility of my new name, my classes filled up within seven days, and my house came back into order. That is how it all works. Accept your livable moment! Do not worry about next week, and always remember that last week is finished. If you are correct in your thinking now, the future is automatically preparing next week, on your behalf. The secret is to keep the mind both pliable and available, through allowing your mind to become the light of your life. In order for you to evolve into your next thought, come back into the moment. It is the vibration of the sound before the word releases that sets the Metaphysical language of the brain into action. We are on this earth to live, love, and become complete – so do not waste a moment of it!

Throughout my training to receive the breath of Shamanism, many Elders from other cultures came to Australia and initiated me into their own tribal laws. Most of these Elders were men who arrived on my doorstep uninvited; I received only four women. Those magnificent people who had also earned their Shamanic experiences, only stayed long enough to give me their gift of consciousness and to initiate me into my new name, which their tribe had bestowed on me, and then they disappeared out of my life as quickly as they had come into it. They came to Australia representing the cultures that had evolved before mine. All of them knew the story of my family tribe and could explain parts of my life to me, which, at that time, I had not yet been made fully aware of.

My Aboriginal name is "Rainbow Wadjinda". That name, through the English interpretation of the Pit-Jan-Jat-Jarra tribe, means "Illumination of the Ocean". If we look at the word "Wadjinda" through the Sacred Alphabet, "Wadi" means "wisdom ascending through the Divine Justice". "Inda" interprets as "intelligence nourishing through Divine Ascension" – or, simply, "to search". When decoded through the Egyptian language, "Wadi" means "serpent". Do you see now how the Aborigines first understood the codes and came to the fruition of the Rainbow Serpent?

Notes:

CHAPTER FOUR

Ages Of The Collective Soul

Now we move on to discover more information regarding the codes of consciousness, through the understanding of how we have learned to release the Sacred Alphabet and the Sanctification of Numbers. Read this next section slowly in order for you to absorb my understanding into accepting the following knowledge. Let us begin with the understanding of the Alpha, Beta through the Art of Astrology.

The Astrological wheel is another tool of reference that connects us into the inner mythological journey. This journey is an added value to your intelligence, which has manifested into its own discernment through your following the mathematics of the Universal Law. Astrology is an introduction into the language of Metaphysics, and it is also an explanation of how we can form a deeper relationship with our Soul's experience – that is, it is a way for us to release a sense of freedom within our self in order to add to, and work with, the experiences that automatically occur in our life. It is the doorway to understanding the first dimension of gathering ourselves into understanding the Collective Mind.

We refer to the list below as the "Ages of the Collective Soul". Let me explain the first sentence to you, and you will see how humanity began to yearn for its freedom, which, in turn, became its truth. The first sign of the Zodiac is Aries; this sign is symbolically known as the introduction into another world, which eternally explains your new thinking to you. It is known to us as "I am" (my intelligence), and it is the story of the newborn child, who is the resurrection from the ashes of the past generation; this is through the relationship to your emotional understanding, which has come through the availability of your tribal intellect.

Please note the numerical age of each sign. From Aries right through to Pisces, we are symbolically looking at the age of man – from birth right through to old age. The earlier your sign, the more innocently you harbor your feelings towards others, where your journey is to learn to release your pent-up emotions. The later your sign, the more difficult your intellectual awareness is; your journey is to not judge others as quickly as you do. You are the learned one of the clan; therefore, you must learn to think in freedom instead of trying to control others' emotions – as well as your own. Don't forget to add the two words my intelligence after the sign that you were born under, as this explains your temple inheritance to you.

SIGN	KNOWN AS	AGE	ELEMENT
Aries	"I am."	1–3 years of age	Fire
Taurus	"I have."	4–7 years	Earth
Gemini	"I think."	9–12 years	Air
Cancer	"I feel."	13–16 years	Water
Leo	"I will."	17–20 years	Fire
Virgo	"I analyse."	21–28 years	Earth
Libra	"I balance."	30–40 years	Air
Scorpio	"I desire."	45–55 years	Water
Sagittarius	"I see."	60–75 years	Fire
Capricorn	"I use."	75–85 years	Earth
Aquarius	"I know."	85–95 years	Air
Pisces	"I believe."	95–100 years	Water

Each one of us has been born through one of the astrological twelve houses of the Wheel of Life; this language is constructed and brought together through the hidden language of our unconscious mind. Our Soul is created mathematically, where it has been designed through the Oracle of our family's past. Once we have accepted the wisdom of our Soul energy –

where we understand the vibrations of what is cast down to us – we are free to conjoin with the next eleven houses, and all this strengthens our Collective Mind. In other words, this is how we learn to become our own arbitrator and be totally responsible for our self.

We are aware, through the strength of the myth, that we have twelve strands to our DNA; metaphorically, this refers to the twelve Apostles, Disciplines, or Disciples that help us weave our web. We have twelve strands that are delivered unto us from above, and these twelve relate to the right hemisphere of the brain. We also have another twelve strands that reach up from our primordial past, which is known as our ego; the ego works in concordance with our left brain, and these other twelve strands relate to it. These twenty-four strands, together, create the double helix of our complete DNA, and both sets of twelve strands must learn to live in a habitual resonance with one another. There are twelve from the light worlds, and twelve from the darkness of our past. The past belongs to the Netherworld; the light worlds are our availability to create our future intelligence to support us along the way.

There are twelve months in one year, and the word "year" was gathered through the Collective to represent: through our "yearning to 'EA' we ascend and release". We also have twelve houses – or wheels – in the worlds of our Astrology, which represent the neural pathways throughout the language of the brain; metaphorically, they represent the star systems. All are one and the same.

Notes:

CHAPTER FIVE

The Language Of The Divine Inheritance

Allow me explain to you another little story. It starts like this: "I am, and so I have to think. I feel in order to will myself to analyse, and this brings me into harmony and balance, giving me a desire to see how to use my knowledge to believe that I am as God is." Remember, we were made in God's likeness. The sentence I created to start the "story" is an explanation of the twelve Astrological signs. (Please also see the list at the end of the previous chapter). This is an explanation of both your evolution and the experiences that you can reconnect to through your DNA – this is the language of the Divine Inheritance of your forefathers and –mothers, which are the collective, tribal memories embedded in your cells.

You were born at a certain time, on a certain day, in a certain month, in a certain year. That is your Astrology. The right brain remembers all the stories that have been stored through the past inheritance of your DNA in regard to how your intelligence has the opportunity to release itself.

Your life evolved through this acceptance of your incantation, which is a hidden language that you were born with; but, through your own innocence, you have not yet fully released or understood it all. Why? Your ego can only connect to the top surface of your storehouse, and so it collects around thirteen words at one time. It likes to skim across the waters, not dive in! It may get its feet wet, but that's about as far as it likes to go. It is like sending someone into your pantry to collect a jar of jam; if that jar is not in the front row, staring the person in their face, he/she cannot find it! Why? That person is looking at the shelf, but he/she is not seeing – or even noticing – what is stored there!

This information is unknown to us on a conscious level, as our storehouse of memories are not available to us until we open them up through the delivery of self conforming to the subconscious self; this will continue to automatically deliver us up into the unconscious mind, which is another explanation of how we can accept that we are made in the likeness (image) of God. In other words, it explains the story of the emotional intelligence of our Soul – and it is beyond our comprehension as to how we understand just what the fullness of our truth has in store for us.

Some say that we came from the stars. However, "ashes to ashes and dust to dust" is the story that most of us have heard. Be aware that this is also exactly how a star is formed through the Laws of the Universe! What is the prayer at a burial? From death comes life, and life is everlasting; from the past, the future is born. Your mythology unfolds in you as you develop your intellect. It is a fractional experience of your self-worthiness, which is cocooned inside you – tucked away in your tribal law. In other words, through the ages of all humanity, this explanation shows us how we can use these stories that are ready to manifest on our behalf. As we think, so, too, do we form our own creation?

Allow me to announce to you another explanation of how we evolved into this understanding. In the Arabic language, the number six (6) interprets as the "mastering of self", and, in English, it is written as sitah, with a silent letter i, so it is pronounced, "stah". This explains to us that the codes connected to the intellect of the mind are reaching for the stars, which are the sparks of light that thread their way through the neural pathways of the brain. We have been informed that the Egyptian text speaks to us through their "song lines" which travel through, or return to, the stars. When we are able to understand that the hieroglyphs are also explaining their royal Metaphysical language, we will receive a different version.

Another example carved or painted in the hieroglyphs are the many horses and chariots. Whereas we think that these are explaining a war being fought somewhere across the empire, they were actually scribed as the ships of the desert, with their arrows in their hands. What is the ship? It is your body! What is the horse? It is your Spiritual strength! What do the humans represent? They are your genes! What are the arrows? They are aiming to change the results of your thinking! Each chariot is one of your thoughts, and, if it looks like a confrontation between chariots, that is where the ego of one thought is overpowering that of another thought! One day, we will correctly interpret those amazing principles!

This is also why the Bible is so hard for us to understand; most of us don't realize that it is simply bringing the story of our evolution together on a conscious level. The biblical references are merely explaining the unconscious language that is embedded throughout your DNA. You see, there are no vowels in the ancient language at the time the Bible was composed (i.e., Hebrew, Aramaic, etc.), which explains the origin of the Arabic language. The vowels in these languages came through the spoken word, which all depended on the intonation of the person who was speaking and explaining their story. The way in which that person brought through his/her pronunciation – and which vowel sprang forth from his/her intellectual mind – is what determined his/her eloquence. Remember that our thoughts are always being measured through the Collective Consciousness; therefore, as we evolve intellectually, our language changes. We are being shown how the secrets of the codes are reaching through us again.

"Heaven" – or "Zion" – is known to us as the top of the head. So, when we bring all that into order through the codes, we are able to understand that songs – or prayers – are sacredly calling to the God within us; not searching for one that is outside our own boundaries. This resonance came to me through my decoding of the Temple of Hathor, where, situated in the left-hand corner on the back wall of the temple, we see the Pharaoh bringing forth his seed from underneath his garment – that seed is in the shape of little stars. That interpretation informed me of the strength of the semen that will create the continuance of our light, which will become our next generation.

Notes:

CHAPTER SIX

The Journey Of The Myth

The journey of the myth is an explanation towards understanding the higher Collective Mind – it is to the journey of our emotional intelligence reaching up for its supplementary income. Once connected, it becomes a directive from the unconscious mind to connect to the subconscious mind of every single person. Through the inner strength that we confidently release through our right brain, it releases the memories that have been genetically implanted into the aura of our cells; from there, it connects through to the inner vision, which becomes the intellectual light of information that the left brain receives. It becomes a story for the innocence that we are all born with – that is, for us to grow up through balancing our thinking in order to reach up and become the adult. Your innocence has to learn to find the strength of what you can accrue with your next positive thought. It is all about bringing your understanding into accepting your action.

Mythology – or "my theology" – is "my Oracle", which is the aura, or the "prespoken" energy of your cells. Mythology is the story of the light that releases from your cells when you equalize and harmonize your thinking; it is your intelligence unfolding itself from within.

Please remember that the brains of each cell are referred to as our "membrane", so your memory bank is an automatic inheritance. Each cell knows everything about you and your previous generations. It is a map of your Collective Consciousness, heralded back to you in order to explain the mathematics of your mind. Through the Italian language, a map is called "atlante" (remember back to the Atlas myth!). The word "Atlantis" was released from the Collective Consciousness through the channelling of Plato, which was brought forth into our intelligence to explain how the mind of the Collective Consciousness heralds itself back to us. Mythology, like Astrology, represents a symbolic journey in which we see through the mind's eye (third eye), rather than with the eyes of our day-to-day thinking; this type of "seeing" helps us understand the hidden knowledge of our laws within, and this explanation is already embedded in our DNA. Allow me to introduce to you how the word "Atlantis" was explained and given to me.

It was back in the '90s, when I had advanced the state of my own grace to where my ego was becoming deficient, and so I had many questions about these kingdoms of our past inheritance. I asked my teacher, "What, and where, is this place that we call Atlantis?" I was sitting in a chair, looking out my front door and taking in the magnificence of the ocean, when my next-door neighbour and his wife walked past my door holding hands. They noticed me, waved, and called out "hello!". I acknowledged their greeting and waved back to them. Turning back to my teacher, I apologized for lifting myself away from my question. He replied, "They represent the lost city of Atlantis." I thought to myself, "Hang on, old girl, you must have got your wires crossed somewhere." I said to him, "Could you repeat that, please? I did not understand that information." I thought that maybe I had shifted my consciousness and was out of alignment. Again, my teacher said, "Those two people walking past represent the lost city of Atlantis. Plato spoke of this city a long time ago. The story exemplifies that all who reigned in this space spoke the same language and lived in the magnitude of their collective light."

There was nothing that the people of Atlantis could not accomplish. Now, supposedly, the city became lost when Atlantis sank into the ocean over 9,000 years ago, disappearing forever. Most of us are familiar with some version of this story. So, now, let me introduce you to this story as it was actually codified. I will begin with the 9,000 years. Through the sacred codes, this alerts us to the sanctification of the number nine (9), which interprets as "the knowing of all; the completion of a world; the death of one world, which allows for the chance to begin again". The sacred codes also alert us to the sanctification of the number zero (0), which represents the Soul. The number 9,000 has three zeros; the number three (3) equates to the mind, and when a number clones itself, it lifts our intellect up into the different dimensions of time so that we can add value to our thoughts. Therefore, the Divinity of these numbers explains to us that, through knowing all that is, we release from the past, which automatically elevates the mind of the Soul.

If you recall, in the beginning of the mythical stories, there was once a great city called Babylon. And all who lived there spoke the same language. As their intelligence unfolded, some of these people began to break away from the original tribe in order to form their own. It all depended on the balance of minds and how the group equated to one another. Other same-minded groups wanted to do the same, and they also walked in different directions. This refers to Noah and his three sons, etc.

Over time, Babylon began to fall, through the population dwindling, and, eventually, no strength remained to uphold the city, as the people all had walked away from the original story to create their own new one, and so the original city was lost. Now those of you who have stepped up into the next level of your inheritance are able to reclaim the original city. My goodness! The Bible was being explained to me in an authorized manner that even I could understand.

So, back I went into my research; the dictionaries came out, and I searched the words so that I could equate my mind with the codes. It came as a revelation when I found "atlante", the Italian translation for the English word "map" – or "atlas" – but, until things had been explained more to me, I kept that information to myself. Years later, when I was offered a beautiful house to lease in Lago Di Como in Northern Italy, I went looking for a map of the area. The man at the news agency explained to me that I needed "atlantes", meaning two different maps of the region, and all those lost years of my searching for confirmation connected and came home to me. The lost city of Atlantis means, metaphorically, those people who have not yet connected to the quest of discovering their inner connection to themselves. They are referred to as "the lost cities". So I had my answer to the question I had asked twelve years before! Isn't this journey into discovering one's self magnificent? Ask, and ye shall receive! This has certainly been a poignant time for me, discovering and exploring all these myths, and I have come to the conclusion that mythology is an ongoing vision that is alive and well in every human's life, moment by existing moment.

Back to that moment of time with my teacher. I had also asked for the answer to the question of the ancient land of Mu, and, just as I did so, a woman walked past my home with a scarf around her head. That woman's family had recently relocated to the area, and they were of the Muslim religion.

It would take many pages for me to decode the works of "Timaeus" and "Critias" (two dialogues by Plato, both describing Atlantis) – when decoded, these names interpret as "the criteria of time" – but I would like to inform you that, through the path of Metaphysics, these dialogues are similar to the collection of the stories that created Noah's Ark. These Greek works explain the social structure of the Atlanteans, which, of course, is the explanation of the strands of the DNA awakening up into the left and right hemispheres of the brain, which seats itself under the temple mind.

Notes:

CHAPTER SEVEN

Babylon And Shambhala

For many years, I had been fascinated with the explanations as to how we first began to utter our inner sounds. Where did those sounds come from? How did we learn to hear, accept, and speak these sounds? I learned that the language of the planet had broken up as human emotional intelligence urged us forward, through our ego enquiring of itself, and that language of the planet became the language of "Bja-ab-EL-on" (Babylon).

Through the passing of time, we began to gather our verse together, which, in turn, grew into a conversation with others, and the tribe to which we belonged began to find a collection of words through listening to one another. A tribe collects itself through living and depending on traversing – or conversing – with one another; that is, through different personalities of separate entities, or energies, releasing and learning to equalize with one another. In other words, we had created a language. I am coming to the conclusion that "Bab-EL-on" and "Bib-EL-on" are expressing how we view our thinking and how we release those feelings. Is this what the word "Babylon" originally meant? To retain the leadership of that tribe, over time, one language became more advanced than the others, and so that tribe's "Babylon" ruled.

It was through my travelling around the planet many times to sit with Elders of different countries, that I became stringently aware of how each land pronounced their thoughts into words. Those words then created their language. We read of the old stories from many cultures – whether Aboriginal, Mayan, Asian, Mesopotamian, etc. – and, from those parallel worlds, which became our future parables, we have been given the opportunity to see through each word, and to release and use these words to our benefit. When we hear a word, its sound vibrates through the mathematics of our DNA, and it is registered with the inner library of the mind, once it has been mirrored into the selective cellular memory; that word then waits to become a reference for us to use as we create and speak every sentence.

Listen to me explain to you the mythical resonance of the ancient city of Shambhala ("Sha-am-bja-ella" or "Sha-am-bja-Allah"). It is an ancient story, which has become a myth; we know that this story has been related orally since time began, and it began to be written down around the tenth century. This city is untouched by the human mind or time, as we know it to be; it stands above the clouds and holds all the secrets of mankind.

There was once a great king who ruled the Hindu empire; his name was Akbja, which also could be written as "Ark–bja", as it is pronounced in the English language. Let me take that name back through the codes of the Collective Consciousness, and pronounce it in its truth: "Akba" or "Ark-hebja", which means "the Ark of the heavenly energy of our Bja".

Again, remember that these languages are spoken backwards to the English language, so another interpretation is that our inner strength or "Bja", is arching up to reach the heavenly energy of home.

The city of Shambhala was supposedly created by King Akba for the God Vishnu (our inner vision), who held the keys to the doorways of the sutras – or as we know them, the Universal Laws – as one of the many interpretations of the Hindu religion has explained this to me. When the word "Vishnu" is interpreted, it relates to how you will understand the new vision you will receive for yourself when you open up your thinking in order to be exalted up into the unconscious mind.

The Mana Pass is the last village in India before we enter into the mountains, and the warrior who is searching for his city of light travels this pass, seeking to reach Shambhala. This name is often interpreted as the "Most Holy Land of Kashmir". To get there, he must cross the Copper Mountains. Copper is the element that we need to release the dis-ease of arthritis, which is created through our stubbornness – that is, our rejection of self, and, more importantly, our rigid thinking. The word "Mana" relates to the nourishment we give to our self.

In the Eli Mi Valley (sounds similar to the stories in the Bible explaining the journey of Eli) lived a Sage named Padma the Wise ("Pa-Di-Ma"), who hid the treasures of wisdom and knowledge in the clouds and placed the recorded history in the Monastery of Hallchi – or the Hall of Chi (the energy). Another familiar name is the Hall of Recognition from the Mayan principles or the Akashic records from the Egyptian principles. (More is explained regarding those worlds further into this book, and, when we bring this story together, you will understand that every story on the planet is exactly the same – it is just spoken and released through a different hum of the language and of our emotional mind.)

The story completes itself with the myth of the Lord of the Underworld, who tries to devour you in order to stop your progress as you tread through your mountains of fear on this path of enlightening the belief of self. And, through my own journey, I can certainly speak of this section of the myth! The story of Shambhala is about humanity searching for and reaching up into the wisdom of the unconscious mind. It is up there, in that space that has no time, where we can create the space we seek – that is where we will be dis-ease free, and where we will understand the inner library of our DNA. Come on, I am already there – so, trust yourself, let go of the past, and search for your own Shambhala!

Notes:

CHAPTER EIGHT

The Sacred Language

Here are some of my explanations to a few words that I have decoded through the Sacred Language.

Palenque: "Pha-EL-AN-Que" is the name of the lid that covered the tomb of the Sun God, Lord Pacal. Pacal is pronounced "Pha-Kha-EL". The lid is a story that relates to the unconscious mind of man; therefore, we must read the story in reverse. This lid is explaining, symbolically, the spaceship that we all become when we have completed our Spiritual Quest and are delivered up into the realms of the unconscious intelligence.

Akashic: Let me break this up into the first time that it was released, and we conversed with one another, referring to it as the "Ark of Ashes". We reverse this title, as it relates to the language of the unconscious mind, as the "Ashes of the Ark". This is known as the Resurrection in the Bible. Another name is the phoenix, the bird rising from the ashes of its own pyre, from the Mayan principles and/or the Asiatic philosophies. It is also known as the Golden Pheasant, and it explains the Book of Revelations. The Ark represents you releasing your past – your DNA – as you birth into the generations of Noah (the "knower of ways").

Land: "EL-AN-DI", in the old language, which means "the body". When decoded, this explains to us that we begin with the God "EL", journeying up to be educated through the God "AN", where we are prepared to reach our Divinity (or the Divine City). My maid in Egypt was about to be married; she informed me that she was journeying to another land, which she called the "Land of the Bja Seth", pronounced with a silent h (Set). Now maybe we will get the story right regarding Seth of the Egyptian principles, who was "set in his ways and would not budge". I had not heard of this area, and so I asked her where this place was situated. Thinking that she was moving to a new land, I asked her where she was going. Was it Ethiopia or Sudan? She explained it to me this way: She was moving away from her tribal home, going to join her husband who lived in the "Land of the Beast". In reality, this was a mere three houses away – but, in her reality, it was an entire world away.

I was amazed to hear the Muslim women speak their truth to me; their desire to temper the beast that would become their husband, and they honestly looked forward to the role that they would have the opportunity to play. This is also the relationship to the beast within us, also known to us as our fear, which we keep re-creating within ourselves when our ego does not want to understand or accept our next evolutionary step of intelligence. I was discovering the way the Arabic language had collected itself, as they still held the codes to the Metaphysical explanations when speaking, which is exactly the same expression used in the Asian languages and the Aboriginal dreamtime, and also how the Germanic language had philosophically collected its own tongue through their understanding of much of the Arabic language. These cultures are still using, in their day to day language, what we of the West are searching for.

Record: To "re-cord". "Re" means "to return back into the light of self" – that is, to the "silver cord", as we symbolically refer to the DNA – or "to reconnect us with our life force". This is the cumulative inheritance of the evolution of man. Now we can realize our truth as to how the Akashic Records have collected that name.

Trident: This is the spear in the right hand of the old man of the sea (Poseidon, Neptune, Triton, etc.). When we take this symbol way back in time, it is not the trident; symbolically, it is representing the horns that relate to the power of the bull, with the penis coming up between both horns. There is nothing negative about these ancient signs; they merely expressed the connivance that our sexual energy plays so wonderfully. We find our freedom, symbolically, through these old explanations of the Gods. Do you see how Michelangelo carved the statue of Moses with the two small horns?

Cappadocea: One of the most fascinating places I have been to in Turkey. Now this is how we spell – or spin – the word. The Turkish pronounce it as "Kha-Pha-Dhak-EA", but the mountain people explain it somewhat differently. They pronounce it as "Papa-Di-Ark-EA". As you can see, the two explanations are slightly behind the more pronounced version that we know (also written as Cappadocia). This land, through the shapes of its rock formations, is an exquisite explanation of the power or penis. These upright carvings, which look like the penis with a cap on its head, have been created by the wind; or, more precisely, the measurement of the energy that holds the land together. Hence, the word "cap"; to the more common language, they look like the father figure. Also in this area are other carvings that have naturally been honed by the wind, where we see animals gathering together, which represent the evolution of the human brain. This area is also known throughout other Arabic nations as "the gathering place for Noah to fill the Ark".

Lah Dhak: A city in Tibet. (In reference to the above paragraph, also provides the same explanation regarding the mountains in Tibet.) The Tibetan pronunciation of this city is "EL-Lagh-Dhak-EA", using different emotions and explanations of the language. Those penis-shaped structures are there for the entire world to see (the same as the structures described above in Cappadocea, Turkey). I have some amazing photos of these structures, as well as the shapes of the animals that have evolved through the Divinity of these hills. As the wind wove its way through the valleys, it created the shapes of the animals that were compatible to the mathematics of the emotional responses of the people who expressed their sexual – or egotistical – language throughout that area. These are the guardians of the "Land of the Penis". God has placed the Soul of our evolution completely around the planet, through the evolution of the species, in order for us to connect and mirror back into our selves. We are the Ark and the animals. They are a reminder of our evolution connecting to the twelve lesser Gods within.

Calcutta: This is Golgotha in the Bible. In the Italian language, it is pronounced as "Kolkotta". Through the codes, this is an explanation of the "gold of God"; it also relates to the philosopher's stone – or the Alchemy of the mind. Nice name isn't it? So why are these people all living under sufferance? They have been drawn to this area; when will their world turn for the better?

Xian: "Chi An". When interpreted, this name is encoded as "the energy of our journey through our education system in order for us to release ourselves up into the next level of God". This is the city where the old Silk Road began. Is this city more powerful than any other? Are all the people here satisfied with their progress? Why are people drawn to these areas? Why do they call it home? We do know that, thousands of years ago, the Pyramids were also built underground, around this area, which is filled with the mythical biblical inheritance in regard to its name.

No matter what country I have visited, I was introduced to someone who still held the codes of long ago; these people were there to remind me of the original story, as it is instilled in their minds, and they, through their inheritance, had never forgotten it.

Chechnya: A place name frequently in the news. Let me speak this name through the codes to see what it tells us about that country. "Che-Che-ANEA" is connected through the relationship to the energy of the two higher Gods. "AN" is through our educational system, which relates to our Soul, and "EA" is through the heavens. Listen to how the locals pronounce the name of their country, and you will hear the voice of their God initiating you into their land.

Every country, city, town, and village has been named through an emotional complement to the language of the Universal Laws. For example, listen to the sound of the word before you look at the spelling of the names of places in ancient Egypt; as we hear from within, so it shall become. You will find those same names in China, India, the Americas, Europe, Polynesia, and also in my own country, Australia. The Aborigines of my isolated continent speak and sound this early language of Babylon. We see how all these countries learned to pronounce their vowels; whether they used an a, e, i, o, or u to create the name, depended on the intelligence of the person who was speaking.

CHAPTER NINE

The Language Of The Divine Babylon

I love the country of Egypt! On one of my earlier trips, we came up the Nile from the area of Sudan, heading towards Luxor, and I realized that the people spoke and pronounced their Arabic language differently. Coming up from the Aswan area and reaching north, there is a word that they pronounce as "Te-Ram-Bja-Ram-Bja". Through the old language, the letter "j" is silent and sounded as a "y". "Terambjarambja" is a word that came from Ethiopia, and it relates to a "house of rest" – that is, a house that we all can find within our own heart, through the Arabic language. Upon finishing work at the end of the day one says, "I will go and find my Terambjarambja." It is an announcement to the self to finding peace through resting the ego of the mind.

The same word is also in the language of the Papua New Guinean natives, who pronounce it as "Te-Ram-Bha-Ram". The word is used for a Spirit House, where one can meet God. In that land, the "h" is silent and sounds like a pause. (Note that the letter "h" has replaced the "j" that is in the Arabic word.)

In the Australian state of New South Wales, a town was given its name through a tribe of Aborigines who lived in the area. They called it the "Good Land", as they tapped their heart, and so it was named "Tumburumba" ("Te-Am-Bja-Ram-Bja"). Was the spelling a mistake on behalf of the person who wrote his/her thesis explaining the Aboriginal language? What happened to that first "r"? My teachings emphasize that there are never any mistakes. We speak to the level of our own intellect, which may differ from others who are ahead or below us. The Aborigines have been claimed to be the first rootstock of humanity, so it is pronounced as to how they heard the word from their inner God in order to form their own language. That is to say, language was delivered to them through listening to their unconscious mind. We have since evolved, and, to our detriment, we have allowed the ego to solidify itself into controlling our mind.

The Aborigines still live in their unconscious energy, as they have already evolved into the chapters of our DNA that we are still busily arguing with. They learned to sound the word and adjust their mind to it, in order for that word to connect back to the Collective, which then allowed them to relate to their spoken word. At the time of their evolution, the first "r" had not been released; it had not yet birthed itself. Were the Aborigines speaking their language before the Arabic connection? If we emphasize the letter "t", we have almost the same sound.

The Australian Aborigines are known to be among the first mythical storytellers; they are much older, in time, through the evolution of their consciousness. They were brilliant teachers for me through my initiation into the journey of Shamanism; through speaking ever so softly, they gently explained to me their tribal law. I had to climb very high, intellectually, staying focused in my mind, in order for me to understand the language of their tribal echo; they took so much time to explain their stories to me, as they were speaking to me through the memories of their unconscious mind.

Every story they explained was through an inner mythical resonance. The point I am coming to here is this: the way in which we hear the word that is brought forth from the unconscious mind, through to the subconscious emotional mind, is also the way in which we learn to pronounce the thought. So we have three different languages from around this planet that say the same word, which represents the same meaning. All of them are stemming from ancient cultures, and none of them have met one another!

Over the years, as I went back into the cultures of time, I heard the same meaning in every language. The word "kiora", in one of the Maori languages of New Zealand, means "farewell". It is also interpreted through the codes of the Egyptian language as "ki", which is sometimes pronounced as "chi". The word "kiora", through the Sacred Alphabet, means "knowing the intelligence of the Oracle, releasing and ascending". The word "oraea" is similar to ora, which means "prayer" in Latin, and it is also understood as the aura, which refers to our energy – or life force – that supplements our daily deeds.

There is a town in the Outback called Kikiora; it, too, was named through the Aboriginal language of the tribe that lived in that area, which is pronounced somewhat differently from the Egyptian and Asian languages. The word "ki" is repeated, so the word is connected through the relationship to the energy of the ora or aura. The name is an emotional thought that they spoke and expressed to each other through their "chi", or "ki" (energy). Isn't it wonderful for us to realize that we are all still speaking the original language that our Collective released to become the language of Babylon?

A little town situated near Kikiora, called Kiakato, is also an Aboriginal word from the same tribe. It is a word that is pronounced in the Sumerian or Arabic language as "Ki-Aka-Tu". The Temple of Kiakatu is a place of worship where one can take one's own mind through to a resting place to release the pressures that are busily creating themselves. It is a house of religiously emptying out the past in order to allow for the new. I also heard that word used in Mali, in reference to the ancient library in Timbuktu. The same name is an area in Ethiopia – or "He-teop-EA" as it is correctly pronounced. Can you sense the reference to the middle of that name? It sounds similar to Cheops ("Chi-Ops"), doesn't it? It is also pronounced as "Ki-ops" and "Siops" through certain other Arabic tribes. Are you feeling comfortable with how the language of the Divine Babylon is still alive and serving us?

The intelligence of man pronounced his sound, through the feelings that came up from his sexuality announcing itself, and then it moved up through to his heart, which we now understand is the first-dimension mind of the God "EL". Man learned to feel when he wanted to speak; this was the culture of the Ancient Ones. So here we have the same name in many different languages spread right across the globe. I was fascinated throughout my journey when, as I walked and heard the stories in each foreign land, I also heard my own Australian Aboriginal language being spoken. Isolation keeps the language intact, through the tribe becoming one Collective Mind; but then another isolated area hears the same sound through their unconscious mind, and this accounts for the seemingly mysterious similarities. It is how we mirror our energy to one another; remember, thought attracts thought!

CHAPTER TEN

The Universal Language Is You Discovering Your Temple Of Light

Let us take a look at the codes and interpretations of some Egyptian names. We begin with the stories of Ramses the Pharaoh, who grew up over three generations of time, not family, and we find his Sun Temple in the south of Egypt, in an area that we now refer to as Abu Simbel – or Sam-bel – which means "same sound". The word "Temp-EL" (temple) means "the energy of the God 'EL'". Each time we hear of Ramses, his intellect has grown as to how he has been measured. His second deliverance was known as "Tut-Ram-Isis". He was finally anointed, through his understanding of self, where his complete name is now an ancient city in the north of Egypt called Pirameses – or "Pi-Ram-Isis". There is Ramses 1, Ramses 2, and, finally, Ramses 3; all of which explains the mythical stories regarding how the three Gods became one! This also represents the pyramidal section of the medulla oblongata in the brain. The word "Ramses" explains to us how our energy releases from the base of our body, and how, through opening up our intelligence, we traverse all the way up to entering into the unconscious mind, which becomes our temple of light. (More is explained further on in this book.)

Now let's take a walk further back in time, to a being who was referred to as "He-Ram-Es", and who, supposedly, was a God before the Egyptians began to record their history. We now understand that the word he is the Asiatic pronunciation for the crown of our head. Bring that story into the ancient myths to a God whom the Greek philosophers named Hermes. Roll your r when you pronounce it. Can you hear the same pronunciation? Herames and Hermes both sound identical, don't they?

Let's listen to the sound of the word "energy": "AN-UR-CHI". The name of the second God we birth is "AN", which is known as the educational centre; that is, where the ego learns to transform. It is situated around the solar plexus region of the body, and it includes our energy up through to the heart.

When we decode and interpret this word it means: "through my education as to the God 'AN', I understand and release, UR, my CHI, which is my life force".

The first city to be named on the planet was "ON", denoting that the Oracle Nourishes us. The second city was named "UR", denoting that it is through us Understanding and Releasing our own intellect.

As time progresses, we find that the interpretation of the word "energy", was also known as "khi" or "kha", and is sometimes pronounced and spelt as chi, cha, or sha. In the Chinese language, it is pronounced "xi", "che", or "she". When we go further back, it was "tze" or "tzu", which meant "you"! "Tzu" became "tza", and then "sha", which was pronounced as "Sa-Ha". The sound of the word is all the same. We led ourselves into expanding this word with the sounds of "kha", "khu", "khe", and "kho", which, when understood, related to Que, or the key to the word of the Great One of the Mayan principles: Que-Tzu-Kho-Ha-At-EL. The word "Que" means "to query or to question one's self". Is this how we chose the word "quest" to mean "a journey of experiencing the self"?

We go to Africa now and look at the word "Tanzania" – or has this word evolved from "Tanz-AN-EA"? When released through the codes, this name means "the dance we create between the Gods 'AN' and 'EA'". We are aware that there are two mountains in that area: Mount Kilimanjaro and Mount Kenya. Kilimanjaro is the highest mountain in Africa, known through the language of the local tribes as "the mountain we walk to weave our light". Close by is Mount Kenya, which is pronounced "Kha-AN-EA"; it is slightly smaller in height than Kilimanjaro. Between these two mountains is where the Great Rift Valley begins, moving up continuously through Ethiopia and Egypt, and then farther up, all the way through to the north of Israel. Mount Kenya is represented as the God "AN", and Mount Kilimanjaro is "EA". As I write this story, I feel as though I have every explorer from the past standing behind me, giving me confirmation to go on and on.

Another explanation for the word "Kilimanjaro" – or "Kilim-AN-Jaro" – is that the word "kilim" means "hand-woven", so, through your own action, you weave your words. "AN" is the God of the Middle Kingdom, where you learn to harmonize your self; "jaro" is an ancient word from the Ethiopian language that means "your Oracle". So this powerful word is explaining to you that, as you weave your words through harmonizing your mind, you release your own Oracle.

Take time out now for a drink of water, as the writings are becoming heavily congested, and they need to be flushed through your system; also take time, for you to have the ability to remember that you have already walked these words. Again, I will remind you that the brain of each cell is called a membrane, a member of your brain; and every ounce of information I am releasing here on these pages is ensconced in your cells. It is also a page of your inner dictionary that belongs in the library that we refer to as your DNA.

Another fascinating word is "Sumatra" – or "Tzu-Ma'at-Rha". When we open up into the codes, we understand that the word "tzu" means "you", and "tzu" has now been changed to "su". So, as we accept the codes to the name Sumatra, it explains to us that, "through the Soul's understanding, we are the Ma'at – or mathematics – of the Rha". Do we now begin to see how the mathematics of the Universe has collected and distributed the energy to create the tsunami for this land? Always, it is busily creating the results of our thinking! This is the Collective Consciousness returning to us our dues – or, would you prefer the word "favours"?

What name we gave to an area depended on the emotions we felt as we viewed the land; this has been ongoing for thousands of years. We change the name of a country or city through the explosion of our intelligence climbing higher; this is our driving force of how we create the experience of connecting up into our unconscious mind. We set ourselves an example – that is, we exemplify our mind. Have we lost Babylon? Not on your life! It is still here, walking through us, through every sound we utter. Where have we heard this language before? How did it reach our ears? The hierarchal Collective Mind traverses through our intelligence, releasing itself through the expediency of our emotions in regard to the thought we have in the moment. The Universal Language is you discovering your temple of light; it is where the three Gods – "EL", "AN", "EA" – meet to become one. And all of this has been created on our own behalf through the sonic sound of the unconscious mind.

Notes:

CHAPTER ELEVEN

The White And Blue Nile

I am living these codes twenty-four hours a day; therefore, I am automatically rephrasing every word that I hear back to its origin of Babylon (or, as I first learned to understand it, "how we 'babble-on'"). Having earned my Divinity – and because I am living in these fields of the Collective Consciousness – I ask that you please endure with me as I try to explain these codes to you; it is so much easier to speak and express them than it is me to write them. When it comes time for me to explain these words to you, I have a tendency to overwrite my words. The important part for you to understand is that, as we hear each spoken word, we break it up into syllables; it is not necessarily how it is written – that is, how we spell it – it is how the sound of each word is registered back into our inner dictionary that matters, because it is there, through our own harmonics, that we feel a sense of security, as we know that this language is a part of our tribal heritage. As we learn to reverse everything we say, we find that it is introducing us up into the intellectual language of the unconsciousness mind. People in many lands write their language from the right to the left.

Let us begin this next part of the book by reviewing the Divinity of God, which has been passed down through our DNA in order for us to observe and understand more fully from the third-dimension of reality. When viewed from above, the Egyptian empire began where two rivers, which look like legs, come into one through the area of Khartoum in the country of Sudan. The White Nile began its journey in Uganda from Lake Victoria (or the "victorious waters of 'EA'"). The Blue Nile, which is the journey of the Soul's experience, began at Lake Tana in Ethiopia. The Ethiopian name for this river is Ab-Hu-EA.

The same name in the Sudanese language is EL-Ba'ar-EL-Azraq. I will explain this last name in a sentence: "Through my everlasting life of the Bja ascending and releasing my first God 'EL', ascends Zeus (who releases the light) to my ark."

Those three languages explain to us, through the codes, how we have evolved; that is, they metaphorically explain where we came from.

The Blue Nile has the monumental task of crossing the almost impenetrable gorges of Ethiopia, which are around 240 miles long, in order to continue its flow. It is around 1,000 miles long, until it joins forces with the White Nile and then flows through to Alexandria. We now see how those two rivers represent the previous generation, known as the Upper Kingdom – or the "kingdom that walked before us". The White Nile represents the achievements of the Oracle, which is an essence that is delivered from the right brain. The Blue Nile is the ego conforming to its own justice in order to attain its royalness, which is the left hemisphere of the brain.

We know, through the codes of body language, that the upper inner thighs are referred to as the "lungs of Consciousness" – or where we learn to breathe the Breath of God. We are named humanity ("HU" through the codes); this is the interpretation of the symbolic reference to the scribes of Egypt. At first, the scribes are kneeling down, but, in later hieroglyphs, they are standing up, usually with their right foot forward, in reference to our emotional mind. Always look for the hidden body language. We slowly release the codes that are embedded in our legs as we are urged to move forward through the autonomic responses of the unconscious mind. It is fascinating to note that the language of the past is ensconced in every cell of every human; also, it relates to our modern language, no matter how it is pronounced. As it has collected in the ancient Arabic language, so it has been rephrased and spoken in our modern day speech.

The God "HU" is one of the earlier languages brought forth to explain the first myths, and it is informing us of ascending into our "heavenly understanding"; the word "heaven" decodes our inner language releasing from our cells, earning its way to the top of our head. Extending this word allows us to create a hue, which is explained as "tinting and colouring"; and this is released from the energy of the mind as it arcs up through our fields of relativity to create our time and space. Explained biblically, it relates to Joseph's coat of many colours. This comes from the creation of the word "chromo", which also indicates tinting and colouring. A further explanation of this is the name we have given to the chromo-zomes, which are those tiny rod-like structures that appear in a cell nucleus during its division, and which are responsible for the characteristics of our inheritance of the DNA. Perhaps we should refer to these as "chromo-zones" (note the spelling).

Let us now go down to where the two rivers meet in the Sudan area. The word "Sudan" – or, as it is pronounced in their language, "Tzu-Di-AN", means that "you desire the intelligence of 'AN'". Those two rivers, the White and the Blue Nile, travel north to join at what was known as "Abhu Sanbel". Let me decode this magical word as it was delivered to us in the first time and explain it to you as "Ab-Hu-Sha-AN-Bja-EL". The "h" is pronounced as a withdrawal of breath, where it creates a pause; the "j" becomes "y" when we offer the correct pronunciation of this very intricate name of this ancient city. This junction of the two rivers is where we begin to breathe in through our "lungs of the consciousness" in order to ignite ourselves into the light of our intelligence – or where we begin the journey to connect to our Collective Mind. The "Ab" is an ancient word describing the "first introduction to our knowledge".

The Sun Temple is in this area, with its four statues relating to Ramses II. The number four (4) decodes as the temple, which is the home of our dark and light worlds. Those four statues are symbolically referring to the balance of both brains that we must achieve to continue into the afterlife! Can you begin to see how the double helix was first explained to us? This, again, is a code of the relationship to the left and right brain coming together, from the beginning of what the Egyptians refer to as the first time. Is it? Or is it the word "Ram-is-is", which could also be interpreted as the "Ram of Isis"?

Look at the word "Genesis", which could have been spelt "Gen-es-is" or "Gen-is-is" (the "generations of Isis"). Or did we understand it as the "Genes-is" – that is, the "Genes of Isis"? What stories were they leaving behind in order for us to birth into the next step of humanity? There are so many ways that we can watch the unfolding of our intelligence, which is given to us through the understanding of this amazingly organized mind of previous people, who knew and recorded for all of us their interpretations of the secrets of the unconscious mind.

Notes:

CHAPTER TWELVE

Luxor – Where The Intellectual Light Of The Oracle Releases

We continue north up the Nile, moving into the area of Luxor, where the intellectual light of the Oracle releases. This area is in the same position as our navel; it houses all the temples and universities, which explain the collected evolution of all their knowledge. Then we traverse up the river to come to the delta, which represents our head; from there, the river meanders out into the Mediterranean Sea. The shape of the Nile is long and narrow, and it looks like the spine of humanity, with the delta (head) at the top. We are finally beginning to understand and accept how those three Gods – "EL", "AN", "EA" – became one!

The people have gathered to live along the banks of this river, as it supplies them with their sustenance and knowledge. As we journey further to the North, we note that the density of the population begins to thicken. Cairo has around 35 million people living in one small area, and that is much more than the total population of Australia. Why are there so many people in this area? What energy drew those people to this city? Why did they have to rely on one another to keep their own home fires burning? What keys were they unconsciously searching for? Those people were drawn to that area through searching for their next step of understanding and earning their hidden knowledge of the unconscious mind.

Craving to advance their own intelligence, they were unconsciously drawn to the area for many reasons (i.e., security; looking for someone to lead them; not wanting to miss out or be left behind; knowing, from somewhere instilled in their being, that this spot represented a sacred place). The same story goes for the explanation of the name of every city that has collected and created itself on the planet. You are attracted to an area for what you are longing to receive in order to find your self-satisfaction. Do you see how the tribes evolved? Through your own forthrightness, you chose to migrate to the same mind. When we fly over

Egypt, through the unconscious mind, we are automatically drawn to the green area of the Delta, as it releases the largest combustible area of energy. That area relates to our brain – or our "heavenly home".

Alexandria ("EL-Ex-AN-Dri-EA") is known throughout the codes as the "city or home of the three Gods", and is situated high up in the delta. It also symbolically represents the crown of the head. It first became famous for its large lighthouse; the story is told that its light could be, and still can be seen, right around the planet. We can add to that previous sentence, much more eloquently, by saying that the lighthouse is also how our thinking releases from the brain back down into our body, which mirrors its reflection out into the aura of self – and, from there, into the Collective, where we become a light that is seen by others.

More recently, Alexandria is known to us for its famous library, which supposedly held thousands of books regarding the evolution of humanity. Did it ever occur in reality; or, as the myths have designed it for us, is it where our thoughts have released out to create what we think is the truth of reality? Do you see how the myth begins? Or, is it just a vision that has been handed down from father to son, mother to daughter? We have to keep going back into understanding our beginnings, so that we can accept our past – and, thereby, be able to release it in order to create our future. Somewhere, long ago, a story began to emerge as the intellect opened up to reveal an image of the pages in the library of the mind. How the story of the intellect unfolded back depended on how focused the mind of individual person was. I remember at the beginning of my journey, as I stumbled my way through these codes that were showing me what I thought at that time, I discovered replicas of the Temples of Knowledge and the Great Halls of Wisdom – and, more importantly, the many hundreds of steps that I had to climb to reach my attainment. I have climbed those steps a thousand times over in order to bring you this information. If I did not get the information right or correct, I tumbled down those stairs, picked myself up, dusted myself down, and started all over again. These magnificent buildings – with their columns of support out in front which supported the forehead of my mind, and the many, many steps – are still here, all around the planet, for all of us to view. I now refer to them as my "parliamentary buildings" – that is, as to how I have balanced my self. In other words, this is how I learned to look through, not at!

For thousands of years, many famous people have searched for the foundation stones of the library in Alexandria. They are still searching, although, along the way, they think they have discovered bits and pieces of the original information. This information was released through the language of the unconscious energy. It is not of the three-dimensional mind. Just like the stories of the Bible, they are explaining this hidden code in a language that is beyond our third dimensional reality and until you step up into your truth or your next realm, you will spend the rest of your life wondering. When the time came for me to leave Europe and return home to write my books, my own country burnt itself into the ground. My tribal pathways had to resurrect themselves for me to continue!

That library supposedly burned to the ground – or so the story goes. Fire is symbolically known to us as the resurrection – the ending of one world to begin another; or, the phoenix rising from the ashes. This is also the story of humanity leaving its third-dimensional reality and moving up into its next step of Divine evolution, where we rely more on the "image inside our nation" – that is, our vision world or our Collective Consciousness – what most of you refer to as your "imagination". This is the land and language of the Hidden God that I am bringing down to explain to you. When you have suffered enough, you will begin to accept the wisdom of trusting yourself to open up your intellect, where you will be delivered up into the realms of freedom.

This story is also informing you of the history of China. The Chinese lived in Alexandria well over three-thousand years ago, staying there for hundreds of years, and travelling and collecting all the information that had been inscribed on the walls and temples. They took the codes of their understanding back to China, where they measured that information into their own language, which in turn created their land.

Every country on the planet desired to collect the information, and so for hundreds of years they have tried to confiscate the information of that "City of Light". Alexandria is the home of the mind, body, and Soul – or the Father, Son, and Holy Spirit. More importantly, it is known as the Library of Elanea ("EL-AN-EA"), which is the ultimate journey of man discovering his self. It is where we, as humans, have the opportunity to earn our royalness of self. Another reminder is that the first dimension of the God "EL" executes itself through its understanding up to the acceptance of the second dimension, which is the God "AN". We call that God the "University", where we educate ourselves into the Middle Kingdom, as it has the responsibility of collecting and housing our acceptance of self; it is the home of our Soul. The world of "AN" opens up and gathers the emotional feelings that release up through our heart, which begins to create the action of our angelic resonance; that is where we begin the path of our Divinity, which was previously known as our Divine Unity, and, through opening our heart to ourselves, we symbolically birth our wings. We return to Egypt, understanding that the hieroglyphs explain this awakening as the woman with her wings outstretched; she is named Ma'at, symbolically representing the mathematics of the mind.

In other words she is representing the one who has opened their heart to understand themselves.

The God "AN" fine-tunes our understanding, and our action then begins to reach up into the third dimension, which begins above our heart around the upper chest, throat, and neck area. The final step now begins, where the positive action of our thoughts creates our conversion of entering up into the home of our sonic sound. We begin to converse into the house of the God "EA", which is known as the "Heavenly Kingdom" and also the "Crown of God". Interesting, isn't it? Those ancient stories of the past were releasing the truth to us, from the beginning of time.

Now you can better understand the "library of the mind" (or inner library), known to us as Elexandriea or Alexandria – the resting place of our own individual inner universe. We are more familiar now with why the cave artists of long ago painted a circle of light around the crown of the head. I am not explaining anything new that is not already embedded in your cellular structure; I am just reminding you that you are the evolution of everything that has been, is, and will be. The word "remind" ("re-mind") means "to return your truth, or your mind, back to you". Every one of us can become our own hero and dwell in our house forever. Please remember, when I open up my heart to believe in me, my light attracts others; this is where I speak to you as "we" or "us".

Notes:

CHAPTER THIRTEEN

The Delta

On the eastern side of the delta is the city of Port Said (previously known as Bor-Tza-He-Ad), which represents the higher forehead. We can understand how the word "head" came down the line. Is this where the word "tzar" (or "tsar") came from? Hear the similarities of the sound when you pronounce "Borzahed" and "Port Said" – one is Arabic, and the other is Greek. Again it is our Collective Inheritance as to how we show our respect to another human being. It is known to us in the language of Metaphysics as the "Cenotaph" or the "Obelisk" of the mind, where we can release the memorial understanding and salute our own mind, as well as each other's.

That same area is also known throughout the Metaphysical resonance as the "vision world" – that is, what most of you nonchalantly call your "imagination", or, as I prefer to call it, the "image inside your nation". It is a language explaining your thoughts back to you. The story of David in the biblical inheritance of "Da-vid-EA" has the same explanation. The word "Davidea", in the Sanskrit language, is interpreted as the "inner teacher". Is this where the word "intuition" came from? Why do we have the word "video"? We place a film into a video machine, which is transferred back to us through the television screen. (More is explained regarding the matter of physics, or Metaphysics, further into this book.)

The city of Tel Aviv, in Israel, is the introduction to our sonic sound; could this have been the forerunner to the creation of the word "television"? It is the doorway of entry into the unconscious mind, which begins at the base of the skull; this is where we are exalted into the unconscious recognition of self, through moving up through the medulla oblongata in the brain, and it is also where we are reminded of the possibilities of earning our "royal chambers". Pay more attention to your inner library, as it has every answer that you are searching for.

The forehead is also known as the home of the unicorn ("eunuch's horn") – or the einhorn ("one horn") in the German language. It is also known as the "horn of plenty" (cornucopia, in Latin) throughout the myths, and the "horn (or 'house') of Horus", throughout the Egyptian philosophies. I will sneak my thoughts in here and explain that I like to refer to this section as the "home of Jesus Christ"! The left brain is Jesus, and the right brain is Christ. Are we rerunning the old movie of our DNA? Are we still trying to catch up with our past?

Cairo was previously called "EL-Kha-He-Rha", which, when decoded means "through everlasting life our knowledge heavenly ascends through to the heavenly energy, and releases us up into heavenly ascension". Wow! Many mentions of heaven here; three, to be exact: one for each level of God. Remember that the word "through" means "seeing from within". What a title! This is a grand commission for the people of Cairo to live up to and call home. Cairo is also referred to as the "home of the Pyramids".

The delta looks like the shape of our brain, and it has about twelve channels of water opening up north of Cairo. Over time, these twelve original channels have divided into other smaller rivers, spreading the waters throughout the delta, which symbolically works in the same way as how our brain "multiplying" itself. In other words, those channels reflect to the twelve meridian lines coming up from the body, which traverse through our DNA and submissively open up into the hypothalamus section of the brain. These channels unfold as we birth, extending our own intelligence as the years of our life are comprehended. Does this sound familiar to you regarding the twelve Apostles or the twelve Disciples? We are beginning to tie up this wonderful evolution of the mind. Watch the story unfold in this next paragraph.

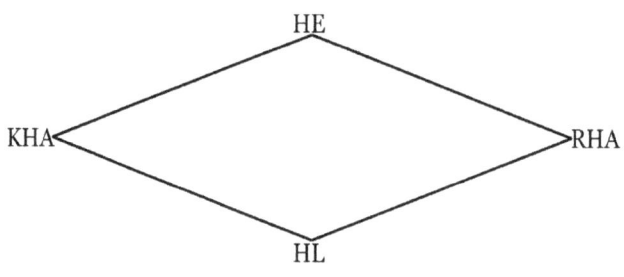

Have you noticed another doorway that is identical to the symbol of the code through the ancient language: "Ma'at-he-Ma'at-ic's", which is explaining the geometrical symbolic structure of the mathematics of the mind? Are we beginning to see how the reality of the brain muses into the "OM"? (Or, to use the word as we know it today, "museum", where we collect the glory of our past.) Also known as the "Oum of Allah", where we take the essence of smoke or receive from the ash into our palace (or place) of worthiness. Is it all becoming clearer now? Can you begin to see how you are rising from your ashes? You are reducing your past, and also the Collective Inheritance of your forefathers and –mothers, which creates an algorithm into your future. Let's give ourselves the "all clear" for our future generations to inherit!

Referring back to my book "Decoding Disease", we can begin to understand that lung cancer has become more prevalent through humanity's not understanding how to give thanks back to the inner self. Unconsciously, we automatically reach up into the Collective for the smoking ritual, which we know will help us stabilize our mind. Why are more smokers not attracting this dis-ease? The mathematical table has swung in the opposite direction, where more non-smokers than smokers are attracting this dis-ease. Why are these people who have adopted a religious ritual, through the ancient smoking ceremony, free of lung cancer?

Through extracting the essence from that herbal resonance, we knew that we could suffice in each moment when our thoughts became overloaded. Unconsciously, we were trying to release our trauma through resurrecting ourselves from the ashes.

It took me quite a number of years to research and understand the importance of this sacred ritual that we return to ourselves through the Shamanistic principles. The inner dragon had to come alive! I had to learn that my ego had to gain its own confidence in order to work with and on my behalf – as opposed to me continually working for it. I had done that for most of my life, and it had continually held me back into an abeyance of self. The child in me had to find the courage to accept adulthood.

We are not meant to swallow or suck the smoke into the lungs. We are meant to siphon and filter the essence of the tobacco plant up through our mouth into the two little holes that we have in the roof of our mouth. Smoking is not meant to be an addiction. We have gathered the mathematics of this resonance to balance and harmonize the ego. It becomes an instalment of an overdue recital. Do you understand, now, how we have symbolically created the mythical dragon, with smoke and fire coming out of its nostrils?

Our body is a huge doorway of Divine intellect. Through the principles of Egypt, the "Kha" is referred to, metaphysically, as the mirror of knowledge that reflects throughout the self – that is, through the relationship that we have with our Oracle. It is the inner knowledge! Autonomically, it creates the action of our right arm, which connects through to our right brain. The "Rha" is the action we release through our left arm, which connects to our left brain. So balance yourself! Lift up your arms and fly right up into your library, which is waiting for you in the upper echelons of your mind. You are embedded with all of it!

Notes:

CHAPTER FOURTEEN

Giza, Saqqara, And Faiyum

A new timeline was emerging in my mind; the more I understood this sacred language, the more I seemed to be opening new doorways of knowledge, where I realized these magnificent carvings are explaining to us the evolution of our mind. This wisdom was mirroring itself back to me, the more my confidence grew. I had a desperate need to understand these ancient superior sciences, and I knew that this could not be rushed or pushed; it would only reveal itself, in all its truth, one step at a time.

This was how I realized that this new chronology I was discovering was proving to me that all this information is much older than we first understood it to be. Please remember that changing the timeline that has been set up previously removes us from the patriarchal connection, which is where we begin to differentiate. We forget that achieving consciousness is our highest order and value of self in regard to why we are here on the planet.

Just below Cairo is Giza, in the ancient language, "Gy-Tzha", which, when decoded, means "God's yearning releases the truth of the 'Zha'". The Chinese have revealed the same name of "Xi Tza", which, when interpreted means "Chi Tzar is the inner energy" – or the life force of the Tza. Also, Tza, in the Chinese language, interprets as "death". This interpretation refracts, depending on the level of speaker's intelligence. They are correct in their assumption that it is the word "death"; not in the sense that someone will die, but rather that the person is ascending in the mind to die to his/her old ways.

The city of Giza represents where the Oracle upgrades its information through the glandular systems at the base of the brain; we refer to this area as the home of the "Py-Rha-Mid-EL" section of the brain. The ancient name of this city was Pi-Ram-Isis, and this is the medical term for where we learn to master our intelligence. This is also the crossover distribution point that we mentioned earlier, where I explained the city of

Abu Simbel and the stories of Ramses.

Just below Giza is the city of Saqqara, which denotes through the codes as "my soul ascends, and I release through my relationship to the quest (note that there are two "qs") and ascend my 'Rha'". The city has been named after the God Sokar – or, more correctly, "Tzo-Kha-Rha". Is this in relationship to that wonderful word, "Ein Tzorph", the Hidden God of the Sacred Law? Sokar represents the Egyptian God of the crow. In Shamanism, the crow – or "Kha-Rha-Ah" in the old language – is known as the "keeper of the sacred law". We use crow feathers to protect our Book of Laws, which is an angelic garment we wear. Is this how the Vedantic Laws of the Indian and Tibetan masters created the word "chakra"?

Crow is known throughout the Shamanic principles as the "police constable" of the Sacred Law, symbolically representing the bird or angelic tribes. Have you ever watched the magnificent crow in action? It builds its nest with the branches that have fallen from trees. When I was out in the desert completing my Shamanic Inheritance, I watched as one crow tried for hours to snap the dead end off a branch that was still connected to the tree. He kept on coming back and repeating the same gesture, and I thought that it was a stupid thing for the bird to do when there were plenty of dead branches already on the ground. At the time, I did not realize that the crow's action was a message for me. I was trying to prove something to myself – something that I had not fully digested – to end a lesson before I had allowed the mathematics to be relayed into an alignment, where the thoughts would seat themselves into the right hemisphere of the brain. Once I had realized my inner message, the crow flew away and never came back to try the same trick again.

When I was in the Outback correlating with the Masters of Time, the crows and another species of birds – which we refer to as Apostle birds, as they collect and fly in groups of twelve – liked to fly inside my dwelling and be with me while I was working; they wanted to connect with my energy. I was living permanently up in my unconscious mind at that time. I was creating my own combustible energy, and that is where their sonic sound finds home. The Apostle birds would become entangled in my hair when they were flying around, and, finally my antenna reached up into its peak, and I shouted out to God, "Enough is enough!" So the birdseed came with the next delivery of groceries, and it helped ease the situation by keeping most of them outside the door. Once I had explained the situation to Crow, he stood silently at the shed door, as if he were a sentinel, and stopped the others from entering into the room.

When I placed out my food scraps along with some seed, I began to become aware that Crow has this uncanny habit of walking around a group of birds, checking to ensure that the share of nourishment each bird received was balanced and harmonized between them. If not, he would march into the circle of birds and give the greedy ones a beating. His wings would encircle that greedy bird, and his feet would march over the bird very quickly; the greedy one was then sent out to the edge of the circle. Crow did not hurt the bird; but the guilty bird was very quickly reminded of its manners, and I watched as the other birds surrendered to Crow's bidding. Through their deference, they soon realized who the boss was! Crow did not eat until the others had their fill. Crow earned the role of the keeper of the sacred laws; through the sun shining on his iridescent black feathers, he completed the colours of the rainbow, shining like an opal and blinding the others.

I have shed many tears at the beauty of the species that have collected in the name of God. Each bird species has earned a rung of Jacob's ladder, and the crow is right up there near the top. The crow is comparable to the Australian currawong, which, in the Aboriginal language, is pronounced "Kha-Rha-Wong". The last syllable of that word is very popular in all the Asiatic languages. How many families have you heard of with Wong as their tribal name (surname)? "Kha-Rha-Wong" is also comparable to eagle. There are so many stories that spring to mind.

We continue on our journey now from Saqqara down to Faiyum, or "Pha- Eoum". Is this where we created the sound of "Aum" (Arabic) – or "OM", as it is known through the Asiatic laws? The interpretation of "Pha-Eoum" is explained through the words of my Arabic Shamanic teacher, whose name was Aladdin (coded as "Allah-He-Ad-AN"). He explained to me that, "Something of great power happens to us somewhere in all our days, as we gather ourselves together." Through the codes, the word "Phaeoum" denotes "through the power of my heaven ascending, I evolve into the Oracle through the understanding of Ma'at". In a condensed form, it is where the twelve Apostles of Christianity begin to release their restriction over our self. It is the energy of the twelve Gods of darkness (the past) and the twelve Gods of light (the future) merging as one; that is, it is how our DNA unfolds itself. In the world of Astrology, as each one of us is born, we are given one of twelve signs through our birthdate, which becomes our foundation; our Quest of Life is to search within in order to release the other eleven. This education teaches us to accepting others as we learn to accept ourselves. It is all starting to sound interesting, isn't it? The Chinese have the eleven Gods that are attached to the temples in China, and each human is the twelfth. Do you see how far ahead of us they are? We also now understand how the stories that were written in the Bible are beginning to release themselves back to us. The Bible is a coded recognition of the evolution of our cells, releasing the truth throughout the whole of humanity.

Notes:

CHAPTER FIFTEEN

Solomon's Temple

Please read the following words slowly in order to open up those inner codes which are embedded in your mind; they are all on standby, waiting to assist you. I would like you to pause here before I share a Metaphysical story regarding Solomon's Temple. Mark the page that you are reading, as you need to take time out to rest the brain. Drink plenty of water to flush through your system. Don't let your mucus collect and gather, through your fear or ego refusing to understand itself; the mucus will set like cement, and you will become very heavy, where your ego, once again, will have complete control over you. This is the home base for the creation of all your future dis-eases. Oh! Don't forget to thank yourself for what you have understood regarding your hierarchical mind so far!

The story unfolds that, in earlier times, Solomon's Temple was supposedly built for Yahweh, who metaphorically represented the God of Lightning. Yahweh sounds like "EA-Way"; some languages pronounce it as "Ave", which could have been the precursor to Ave Maria. It is also similar in pronunciation to the German word "Affe", which is the ape-like God of Egypt, who symbolically represents our ancient primal force of energy. It is the precursor to human evolution; the primordial reasoning of one of the first God's of power; through our ego learning to understand itself. Yahweh is announcing to us how we can use our intelligence to ascend ourselves up into our own light. This magnificent God is also referred to as the God Zeus in the Greek philosophies and myths. The name changed according to the emotional language that we released at that time.

The Old Testament explains that Solomon became the King of Israel. He was the second son of King David and his wife, Bathsheba. Let us look at the codes to understand this word "Bathsheba". The "bat" sits at the base of the brain (remember that it is known to us through the Shamanic laws as the sphenoid bone). "She" (or "chi") we now know relates to our inner energy, and we know that the "Bja" is the tribal strength that we carry in our bones – the storehouse where we inherit the fear that was trapped in our past generations, through their innocence of not understanding themselves. Metaphorically, Bathsheba represents the emotional balance of the inner screen, which is tucked away behind our forehead.

Through the codes, the number two (2) represents "relationship". The first son could not inherit, as he was jealous of his brother's thinking; therefore, he would not release his inner strength. David chose Solomon to inherit the lineage. The ancient religions describe Solomon as the "wise one"; he was in charge of all the sages (the "Soul's ages"), and he had the power to be in charge of the spirits of the inner realms, which are those that we cannot see.

Solomon inherited his wisdom from his parents, and, in due time, he became the next King of Israel. He was then informed by God to build two houses. He designed "a house for the name of the Lord" (i.e., for the left brain) and "a house for his kingdom" (i.e., for the right brain). The house for the name of the lord was for himself, and the house for his kingdom represented every personality who lived in Israel. Read 2 Chronicles, chapter 2 (in the Old Testament), and then please go on to read the next few chapters; the story is explained much more easily and clearly there than it is in the writings in 1 Kings, chapters 5–8.

Symbolically, Israel represents the home of all your responsibilities. The word "Israel", through the Sacred Alphabet, means "through the intelligence of the Soul we release and ascend our everlasting life". The kingdom of "Israel" begins in the upper area of the neck, where all our "master glands" congregate. Our thinking cannot mathematically become relevant until it has passed through these master systems; they make sure we take responsibility for what we think and speak before we are able to enter into the energy of "Is-ra-EL". It is similar to sitting for exams at university. The cities of this land are the key points of light – or intelligence – that represent this Promised Land. Israel, through the sacred language, represents the sonic sound; it is the doorway we walk through in order to be introduced into the realms of the unconscious mind.

One of Solomon's first commands was to divide Israel into twelve areas, with twelve officers reigning over each one. It was their responsibility to provide victuals for the king and his household: "Each man his month made provision" (1 Kings 4:7). Here, "household" is interpreted as the king's body.

Allow me to explain the Metaphysical language to you in another way: Those twelve officers were responsible for gathering together the information of the mind – or the nourishment for the king and all who dwelt within. Each officer represented one of the twelve strands of the DNA. That story is similar to the twelve Apostles who went out and gathered the people to attend the sermons of Jesus Christ. We can see more clearly how the world of Astrology was brought into our psyche. As it is out there, so it is within.

Solomon gathered the Canaanites who lived in his land (his body) – that is, who were a gathering of personalities that decided to stay together in order to form their own tribe. They formed an alliance with their king, who was known as Hiram, King of Tyre. When we take the word "Tyre" back into the ancient ways, it was pronounced "tur". "Tur" is interpreted as "door", so his name is deciphered as Hiram, King of the Door. The "High-Ram" – or the power releasing from our innocence, metaphorically represents the sheep. The species of sheep, through the Shamanic reference, represent our innocence; they like to be led.

Let us descend a moment and take the word "Abif" back into the codes. Abif is pronounced "Abu-phi", and, through the codes of the Sacred Alphabet, it means "ascending and balancing through understanding the power of my heavenly intelligence". The letters "p" and "h" are replacing the elements of the whole; "p" for "power" and "h" for "heaven". Abif later became the name of Hiram Abif, who is represented as the master builder of the Masonic temple. So now we begin to see how the stories of the myths collect and come together.

Solomon had difficulty in paying the wages for building his Temple, so he had to raise the taxes – or the tithing – in order to accommodate the King of Tyre's commission. In other words, he had to believe more strongly in himself. He also paid three tons of his own gold (the results of his higher intelligence – or mind), in advance, so that the building could commence. After finding ruins under the site he had chosen, Solomon went in search of another. He chose a place called Mount Moriah – or was it Maria or Murea (the "ancient land of Mu releasing the 'EA'")? Maybe it could represent the Meer of "EA", which is the "ocean of 'EA'". In other words, Solomon moved his plans from the left brain, where the old temple lay, to the right brain, which we know is responsible for our inner emotions. So, once again, we understand that the Temple of Solomon – or the Solo-Man – has been brought inside the self; it is not a relic which was constructed from the past.

Through deciphering the codes, I went into Solomon's life to find that his first love – or lover – was introduced to us as the Queen of Sheba. His mother's name was "Bath-Sheba", so the name presented itself again in relationship to him. The story sounds similar to Jesus and the two Marys (his mother and Mary Magdalene).

The Queen of Ethiopia's name was pronounced as "She-bja" or "Chi-bja". The story says that she had heard of the fame of King Solomon, and she came to prove his wisdom by asking him hard questions – so says the brief interpretation in the Bible. Solomon answered her questions, as he had nothing to hide. She showered him with 120 talents of gold and spices, and she brought forth incense and precious stones from her own kingdom for him. Her 120 talents represented her truth, and, through the codes, the number 120 interprets as "I am the relationship of my Soul". Her gold represented the wisdom that she had earned; her spices represented the inner strength of her thoughts; her incense represented her sexual prowess; finally, her precious stones represented the results of her own thinking – in other words, they represented the crown that she had earned.

Sheba was known to bring riches to men through the way she lived her life; she asked many questions and satisfied all desires. Solomon had never received such abundance from a woman before. She gave him the ships of Hiram that had brought the gold from Ophir, and she also gave him the great Al-mug trees that Solomon had never seen before. I love this part as it explains nicely how she introduced him into other worlds of her own knowledge.

Through the myths of Ethiopia, this wonder-woman was known to have had her left leg covered in hair like that of an animal, and she also had a cloven hoof – hence, her sexual desire. Solomon repaid her by gifting all of her desires, and he gave her whatever she asked for from his royal bounty.

She fell in love with Solomon, and he gave her a ring, as he wanted them to join with one another in a union. Once she took the ring, she became pregnant by him. Again, we see the marriage of the mind – that is, as to how they produced their next thought. Sheba returned home, and, after a time, birthed a boy child who became the first King of Ethiopia. His name was "Men-EL-ic". Remember that the word "men" through the ancient language, is the Sanskrit word for genes. "Menelic" denotes "from the genes of 'EL', I am the intelligence of creation". That's a nice way of explaining Solomon and Sheba's liaison with one another, isn't it?

Let us decode the words "Bathsheba" and "Sheba". Bathsheba is pronounced "Ba-at-chi-bja", who was of a higher caste than Sheba; hence, the word "bat", showing us that she was from a previous generation of Solomon's tribe (i.e., his mother). The "Bja" belongs to the bestial side of us; it is the left brain desiring and coercing to demand satisfaction through wanting control of others; it is our sexual energy enforcing and demanding the release of self. It is also our recorded DNA that is embedded in our bones. This is what gave us our strength in the first place; it is where we learned to stand upright.

Sheba – or "Chi-bja" – his lover, represents the same story; it is the first step to the marriage of the mind.

My old Ethiopian professor friend in Luxor told me a story about Solomon, and he pronounced the name, through the Arabic language, as "Suilimon" – or "Tzu-Eli-Mon", and, when interpreted, "Tzu" means "you". The word "Eli" denotes as the "High Priest who belonged to the first God's intelligence" (i.e., "EL"). Mon means "mastering the Oracle through nourishing the self". He explained to me, according to one of the old Arabic myths, that, in the area where Solomon had chosen to build his temple, he found, to his detriment, the ruins of the old Temple of Enoch. Through my interpretation of the codes, the word "Enoch" (spelt "Eunuch" and pronounced "Oinuch" in the German language) is also the word "eunuch" in English.

Now read the following sentences, and let us set this story right. A eunuch is supposed to have had his sexual area castrated – which was meant to curb his sexual appetite – as the Elders felt that he was safe to have around women and could not make them pregnant. He had lost his urge to procreate and had opened up into his feminine mind, where he became emotionally balanced. Enoch's tribe – or caste – has been rated through the expediency of his intelligence, opening up into the power of his temple mind; hence, the word "castrated"; in other words, his "caste was rated".

What we are beginning to understand is that his sexual overtones had evolved up into his educated mind, where he had no need to exploit his sexuality. He found that he could absorb his sexual energy, so that it could be used to transfer his intelligence up into his own kingdom; in other words, so that his inner strength could support him. So now we can begin to understand how the ancient ones collected their own interpretation of the myth of Enoch, whose cast (intelligence) was rated by God; this is how they have explained the message which has been passed down to the next generation. We will leave the removal of his testicles out of the story.

We can begin to understand why Enoch had chosen to construct his temple in the left brain: It was for the freedom and evolution of his ego. Hopefully, you can understand the stories in the Bible through the power of the words, which are few regarding Enoch. The name Enoch also means "greatness" (Genesis 5:24), which explains his Godliness; and, again, in Hebrews 11:5, which speaks of his faith; his story is completed with his prophecy in Jude 14.

One of the codes, which brings the wisdom of the quest, to our attention, says, "We have no need to control others, when our voice overpowers our sexuality." We have created these vices through the detriment of self acclaim – that is, through not understanding the deliverance that came from God in the first place.

Please remember that we are all nourished by our Soul, as to how – or what – we rely on to make ourselves feel comfortable. That is, until we learn to understand our self.

Notes:

CHAPTER SIXTEEN

The Sacred Journey Into The Unconscious Realms

Concubines and eunuchs belong to the higher mind, and they represent the entrance into the Divinity of self. How did these myths come about? When we go back into the tribal laws of long ago, the "head-man" – or chief – was given the respect of breaking the hymen of all the virgins in his tribe. This law kept the Elder's energy in peak performance. His inner strength needed his emotional support. As time progressed, he gathered concubines to him, as he believed he had to keep up his power, which was formed through a conglomeration of his sexuality reaching its peak performance – supposedly, in order to have the strength to be in charge of his people. Now we can understand and see how he needed the extra support from his emotional factors of self to service him, through the understanding of our intelligence during that first time.

Let me go on to explain the codes of whores and prostitutes, which are also written about in the Bible. They are emotional aspects of self that are looking for – or demanding – attention. We use that blatant desire to coerce with other personalities of self, through us not wanting to accept the responsibility of tithing to self. We bide our time and place responsibility onto those other aspects, so that we can use them for our own desire; in that way, we think that no responsibility is attached to earning our learning.

Some of the lower animal kingdoms have many mates; through their evolution, as one species overtook the other and advanced intellectually, they became the higher caste, and, through the diminishment of their ego, they then required the service of only one. It all depends on the emotional intellect that we release as to how our intelligence unfolds when we take more responsibility for ourselves; our sexuality takes second place, as we are finding our sexual satisfaction within. The more we come home to self, the more we move up our own ladder of intelligence. Remember Genesis 7:2, "Of every clean beast thou shalt take to thee by sevens, the male and his female: and of the beasts that are not clean by two, the male and his female." Of the seven, there is one set for each of our seals; as our intellect evolves, we can use these principal species to help purify our inner self.

As it is with the animals, so it is the same with the bird tribes – the more innocent the mind, the more they have searched for added support from the female, and so their mating habits require that extra service. In other words, as each bird species became more intellectually evolved, their ritual of gestation only needed the support of one. Hence, the crow and other black and white birds; also the goose and swan, as we know these species mate for life.

Now you can understand the writings of Schwalla De Lubitz, who wrote "The Temple of Man". He reported on his faithful years of searching for the codes on the floor of the Temple of Luxor. One of his prime interests was to understand the mosaic that he discovered, where the penis came out from the navel. This symbolic pharaonic figure was created to inform us of his advancement when he entered up into the middle kingdom of his mind. It is where the sexual act was no longer a priority for him; which, of course, is when we have succumbed to the word "control", and have achieved the educated mind. The mosaic is explaining to us, symbolically, how the penis is attending its education to receive its university diploma. Now you can understand the story of Enoch in its completeness. In the upper section of that same temple, there was another mosaic that he also discovered, where the Pharaoh had the top of his head removed, and it was open to the heavens.

My explanation of this interpretation is that he had earned his freedom through opening his heart to himself, to discover the laws of his own inner universe, without restrictions or boundaries. He had entered up into the worlds of his unconscious mind, where no interruptions remain in his ego, and where his emotional intelligence would have the priority right to always walk before him. He was free to plug into the Collective Consciousness in order to always receive the truth, through having earned that last step that we acclaim before total enlightenment completes us by allowing wisdom to reign supreme. This is explaining the sacred journey into the unconscious realms, which is the education of becoming the Shaman.

Notes:

CHAPTER SEVENTEEN

Akhenaton

The supposed last Pharaoh was named Akhenaton, and we find that he has been defaced from the walls in Egypt through the Coptic interpretation of Christianity. At that time, they had not yet grown up enough to understand the levels of intellect that he had evolved up into. It is up to the individual to add to his/her intelligence. He was the holiest man of all, through the writings on the wall; he became married to himself, and, when we look at the shape of his body, we see that he is symbolically representing half-woman and half-man.

Through him measuring his own mind up into the heavenly energy – or the crown of the head – he had opened his heart to himself and was a complete manifestation of God. "Ark-he-nat-on" went through his night – or netherworld– in order to find his own light, and he had earned his balanced mind. The Aramaic language has pronounced Akhenaton as "Ayanatun" or "'EA'-nat-on". "EA"'s nation of light. Wow! Now this information changes the original story!

Through the evolution of the myth, the first city that Akhenaton created was supposedly called "ON". The other was known as "UR", as to how we understand our intelligence and release the freedom of the Divine self. He then went on to build the city of Amarnia (or the "Amen of 'EA'", as the words "Amen", "Amon", or "Amun" all come through the heart when it is opened to the self. This city has been created around the heart area as we look down from above on to the river Nile. Remember the river Nile represents the spine of humanity and Luxor is the navel which houses the universities and temples, where we receive our gestation of intelligence. Hence, when we say our prayers or sing a hymn, we end with "Amen". He was the last of the pharaonic kings to achieve the gift of representing and explaining the completed story of humanity's journey into enlightenment, which many of you term the "afterlife". Do you see how we have collected the information that "Tut-Ankh-Amon" (or "-Amun"; also known as Tutankhamen) became the Golden Pharaoh of Akhenaton?

He is representing the intelligence of the unconscious mind – hence, the golden mask. And, if we take a look at the mask that was placed over the young king's head, viewing it from the rear, we see how they have placed the alphabet of both the left and right hemispheres of his brain in blue and gold stripes. As the headdress is collected around the back of the neck, we see how the tail is bound symbolically to represent our vertebrae! It is representing our own DNA, as to how it traverses up into the higher mind. Now that we understand the gift of the Oracle, it has become the evolution for all of humanity to follow "ON", right up to this present day. Or could it have meant the journey of the "Solo-Man", whom we have named Solomon?

Notes:

CHAPTER EIGHTEEN

Tomb KV-63

In addition to all the information I've already explained, I would like to bring things up to date by explaining the codes of Tomb KV-63, before I forget to mention them to you (this tomb was discovered in 2005–06). Situated 33 meters away from the tomb of Tutankhamen, the contents of this tomb included seven coffins (five of which were open and covered in pitch) and twenty-eight white canopic jars that were sealed with plaster and mud. Five of these jars stood near the tomb's entrance of the tomb; once removed and opened, they revealed dust, a carved wooden head of a cobra, and, finally, a shard of pottery from a wine jar. This shard's inscription announced to us that the wine was made in the fifth year for the Pharaoh. The first eleven jars revealed nothing additional. When the archaeologists opened the twelfth jar, they found a seal; the hieroglyphs on it revealed the words "Pa-Aton", which is similar to an inscription on one of the seals found in Tutankhamen's tomb.

Further back into KV-63, they unearthed jars that were filled with human organs (I do not know which ones, but canopic jars were used to hold the organs) that had been saturated in natron, which is salt used for purification. On one of the alabaster jars bore the words "Life eternal" – or "Eternal life", if interpreted through my sublimation; this was a faint inscription, but that, together with the "Pa-Aton", caused the archaeologists in charge to believe that the two tombs are somehow connected.

When the coffins were finally brought to the surface, five of them were open and covered in pitch (as I mentioned) – these five all were filled with sacks of natron, some of which appeared to be small, wrapped bundles. Inside the fifth coffin, they found a small coffin of gold leaf, representing the female form. This smaller coffin had been placed underneath three large sacks of natron. They were protecting the last two sealed coffins; one was in adult form, and the last one represented a child. Both of them were empty. In order to bring this information back to you, please allow me to explain the Metaphysical language of these codes. We are aware, that every tomb unearthed is explaining a story regarding the unfolding of your genetic inheritance. The whole of Egypt is releasing the inner education that we each can accept, regarding the written words that are scribed in our genes; that is, all is explaining eternal life – or, through the unconscious language, all is announcing to us that our life continues!

The seven coffins symbolically represent the seven seals; once we ascend up into the next education of the Universal Laws, these seals have served their purpose in the body. Five of these coffins were already open, as these five represent the freedom earned – or, through the Egyptian philosophies, these five explain the written word, as inscribed in the Book of the Dead, which describes the five free days we earn in order to become the enlightened one.

Let us bring in some more information here. In the Egyptian Book of the Dead, we take note that the fifth plate has no written words; all we see is a single illustration of one Deity, who has ascended totally up into the unconscious mind – he is sitting on his throne above the consciousness, which is represented by water. Now we can see more clearly why there is no need for any text, as the illustration informs us of the freedom that he has earned!

Now back to the fifth coffin, which contained the small coffin of gold leaf in the shape of the female form. This female form symbolically represents the next emotional thought, which, of course, comes through the right hemisphere of the brain, not the left.

All these coffins were empty; therefore, they represent the past. The location of this tomb, merely confirms its support of the story of the Golden Pharaoh. Also the equipment needed to prepare this wonderful effigy for us to extol. It is another parallel that explains the wisdom of his achievements; that is, the way in which he accomplished his inner story. This tomb explains an extra version of the story, though – that is, how we enter up into the unconscious mind through attaining the education of entering up into the royalness of self. Remember that there has never been a mistake; all will be revealed to you, if you create the time to unearth these codes.

The last two of the seven coffins were closed; one of these represented an adult, and the final one unearthed represented a child. Both these coffins explain to us the continuation of our momentary thought; they announce to us that our next positive thought is represented by the coffin of the forthcoming child.

Regarding the twenty-eight jars, we note the mathematical codes: $4 \times 7 = 28$. In other words, we are informed, mathematically, of the tomb releasing to us; the seven seals that are closed to us at birth open up through the education we have reached in order to attain our temple mind! One of the canopic jars revealed a cobra's head and a seal inscribed with the name "Pa-Aton". Was this head representing the twenty-eight cobras painted on the top row of the illustration of plate number five in the Egyptian Book of the Dead? Was the word "Pa-Aton" also used to represent the sun, which was passed on to us, through the Amarna period, in relationship to Akhenaton and his wife, Nefertiti? It is exciting for me to reveal these ancient stories that have been kept within me for many years, seeing them unfold before me as I explain the journey through the codes!

When viewed through the eye of a bird – or, maybe through the eye of Horus – as it flies up from the south, following the Nile and heading towards the Pyramids, the city where Tomb KV-63 was found is situated in the area around the human heart (remember that this part of the world represents the human body, with the Nile as the spine). Remember that, through the codes, the city was released when the human intellect walked up through the heart area; all of which explains to us why the building in the centre of the Great Pyramid is explaining to us the preciousness of our own heart. It is not a tomb for the Pharaoh! Situated above this small building is the five-block-high temple, which has been constructed to protect the heart. Could this temple represent the thymus gland, where we begin to earn our five free days? As we journey through the thymus gland, we are aware that this is the area where the ego is devoured, losing its control over our thoughts, as it no longer has any breath to interrupt our future ever again. When we speak through our heart, we are viewing everything through the eye of the complete mind – our third eye – where we emit our jurisdiction back throughout ourselves! This autonomically creates the intellect we use when we speak with others!

Our newly found wisdom will create for us the Pharaoh Akhenaton, the first Pharaoh to attain a balanced mind, through which he was able to enter up into the unconscious home of God. Now that you can understand the Metaphysical language in its clarity, the word "PA'ATON" symbolically represents our pineal gland – or, as it is known through the Egyptian principles, the Sun God "Rha". Through the biblical period, this is where we see through the Eye of God in order to release the language of the Gods!

As the story unfolds throughout our history, we can find many different explanations; again, this was due to the intellectualization of all the collective personalities of the orator. It took many years of trial and error for me to bring the complex hieroglyphic resonances up into a climax of self-recognition. Here is another explanation that changed as we evolved. Through our intellect, the name of the old Egyptian city of "ON" was changed, and it became known as "Materaya" – or "Mater-EA". The name Materaya is spread right across the planet in many countries; it was interpreted to us as the "Symbolic Death" of our three-dimensional-mindedness as it journeyed up into the fourth dimension of time. It was again changed to Heliopolis by the Greeks (meaning "to spiral up; to bring both brains together"), when they invaded the region and subsumed the Egyptian principles. The word is also represented in the name of the Metaphysical resonance as Lord Matreaea – or "Ma'at-UR-Ra-EA". How did they come up with this name for what is now known as Saqqara – or previously known as Sokar? The journey of the crow! Please relate to the Grecian stories of Apollo, as he was also known to be the crow.

Allow me to further explain the word "Heliopolis". From the Greek, we can interpret this as "city of the sun", but this does not reflect the sacred codes, which denote "heli" as "spiral" (i.e., "helix"). A "heli-copter" flies by means of four blades becoming one – that is, a spiral – which, in the Shamanistic language, represents the power of our energy releasing itself from the double helix of the DNA, through the two spirals of the heart, in order to absorb the ego. All this lifts our energy up through to the pyramidal section of the medulla oblongata of the brain. This, my precious readers, is where we enter the doorway to attain everlasting life! And this is also where both brains meld as one! The next time you see a helicopter overhead remember exactly what you are thinking about; it has appeared to you through the symbolic resonance in order to give you the confidence to go on with that thought you are balancing and releasing in the moment. We are never left to walk alone.

Wonderful, isn't it? In order to collect this information in some semblance of order, there were many times when my mind became so caught up with storing so much information, that I was screaming for myself to stop and forget it all! That is when I would remember something someone once said to me when I first made my commitment to unravel these codes of consciousness: "In any situation, if life becomes too difficult, use the difficulty to get you out of the situation. If it is there in front of you, you have collected it, through its hearing your previous thoughts." The other thing to remember, of course, is similar; and that is my ongoing explanation to you, to reverse every thought you are thinking in the moment in order to release the answer. I can honestly say to you now, as I look back, that I enjoyed the stress that rocked, rolled, and surged through my body for years. And now I am enjoying bringing this compendium together for you, precious reader, in order to explain the mythical ledger relating to the accountancy of the Soul.

"Water, water, water!" is the message that I am being given while writing this. Your lymphatic system is working in overdrive, so please drink to baptize your cells!

CHAPTER NINETEEN

How We Unweave The Threads Of Our DNA

The God Gudea supposedly lived 1,200 years before Moses; Ningursu was his principal Deity. The Aborigines of my land, as well as the Aramaics, have the word "Gudea" in their language. Through my language, Gudea's Deity was pronounced as "Ng-UR-sah", which is a word that relates to the crown of your head. It is a compliment when they pat you on the head and say, "You have a good mind."

We Aussies announce ourselves to one another by saying, "G'Day, mate! How are you going?" In its correctness, we are welcoming that person by saluting the angelic names of the God "EA", as well as Ma'at! What about the name of "Judea", which also is a statement denoting that "you are the Divine 'EA'". By pronouncing this word, we release an announcement to those people listening to our greeting that we invite them to step forward through acknowledging themselves.

The Aramaic languages had a Divine bird that carried a ball of string and a measuring rod; this bird was referred to as "Ezekiel" – or, through the stories of the first time, it was pronounced as "He-Ze-Ki-EL". We read of the same references in the biblical story of Ezekiel (from chapter 2 right through to chapter 20).

Those stories explain the wheels within wheels, which are known to us through the Laws of Shamanism as how we unweave the threads of our DNA. The Book of Ezekiel explains the stories written to the son of man (which, through the Shamanic language, we interpret as, "the power of your next thought") as to how God spoke to him in order to prepare him for his next futuristic thought. Once we understand the preciousness of self, the true meaning of the book becomes clear; it goes on to teach us how to release that innocence in regard to the stumbling blocks that we have inherited, and still hold onto, for fear of losing our self! It teaches us how to awaken and lead ourselves up into the next intellectual level.

The Egyptians – or the Arabic language – have explained, symbolically, that the Divine bird is Thoth, who held the tools in his hands that let us know he was also the Divine architect. When we hear and align with the past, we know the future. The Divine bird, through the Chinese principles, is the crane that lives on top of the mountains and knows all; its name is "HE" (pronounced "her"). Look again at the word "mathematics" – "Ma'at- HE–Ma'at-ic's". Do you see how these words are in relationship to the evolution of you? Those stories all manifest through collecting the matter of physics (Metaphysics) in order to teach you how to open up your own heavenly gates – or, to bring this more up to date, the "stargate", your city within.

Stop looking outside! Look within, and listen to your own sound. This city that you are earning is written in the last verse in Ezekiel 48:35, "It was around 18,000 measures: and the name of the city from that day shall be, 'The Lord is there'." It is within you. How many years was Jesus missing to claim his intellectual light?

Notes:

CHAPTER TWENTY

The Old Aramaic Story Of Aladdin And The Lamp

Let us rest and relax the mind with a small story. It is the old Aramaic story of Aladdin and the lamp, as told to me by my old Egyptian professor:

A young man named Aladdin went to the city looking for an important position. He sought to earn some money so that he could return to his village and live the life of a prosperous man, helping all concerned. As time moved, on he kept looking for work, but he found that no one wanted to employ him. Walking through alleyways he became destitute in his mind; he realized that he had no money left after spending it all on buying food and looking for work. He looked for a place to lie down for the night, having decided that, when the sun rose in the morning, he would turn around and head for home.

Upon awakening, he walked towards the well to wash and refresh, and he tripped and stumbled over something lying on the ground. Aladdin bent down to discover a dull and dirty old lamp lying between his feet. He picked it up, using the sleeve of his garment (remember that your garment, symbolically, is your mind, and the sleeve represents your action) to rub the lamp. He wanted to see if it would become clean enough to sell in exchange for some food. As he rubbed the lamp, Aladdin noticed that he could see his reflection smiling back at him, so he began to rub harder. The lamp was becoming warmer to his touch. Again, he rubbed it; this time, he was aware of a plume of smoke coming from the spout of the lamp. The smoke became thicker, and it began reaching up towards the sky (he was resurrecting himself).

Aladdin was amazed at what was transpiring right before his eyes. He cried out to Allah, "What have I done? What is this all about?" He rubbed the lamp with all the force that he could muster, and, when he had no energy left, the smoke parted to reveal a huge genie, smiling down at him. "Who are you?" Aladdin cried out. The genie smiled and said, "I am a reflection of you, and I am here to serve you. I am at your command, and I will grant you three wishes. If you wish for them correctly, you will never have to ask again!"

Those three wishes represented the opening of the Mind of God; they were the doors of "EL", "AN", and "EA". The rest of the story is simple; Aladdin grew up to collect the crystals that were buried deep inside of him – that is, the inner crystals of his mind. Those gems became brighter and brighter, exalting him up into his own heavenly realms, where the crown he could wear had, embedded in it, all the colours of the rainbow.

The deciphering of this old story is also simple. When the worlds of our emotions are fused together and diminish, our mind becomes most vulnerable. We feel destitute, and can find no courage to assert us to go on; as a result, the Laws of the Universe present themselves to offer us our next step. You see, that genie is the combination of all your genes, which Divinely inform you that they are here to serve you. They are at your command, to help you prepare for your next positive thought.

Notes:

CHAPTER TWENTY ONE

Grecian Stories Through The Metaphysical Language

Let us now decode a few Grecian stories, through the Metaphysical language, where we can begin to see how the Babylonian principles changed through the pronunciation of our thoughts. I would like to introduce you into the understanding of the codes of the God Cronus, one of the first mythical Gods of Greece. The similarities of this story are equivalent, in the Metaphysical language, to the stories of the Pharaohs of Egypt.

Cronus was the son of Mother Earth. He represents the energetic intellectual light of the earth, which, we now understand, represents our body. Through learning our education, we begin to act intelligently; we begin to extol virtuously in order to receive our next positive thought. (Do you see how the language is changing and bringing us up into the three evolutions of God?) Uranus, the father of Cronus, represented the sky. Listen now to the next part of the story: Cronus castrated his father; in other words, his father's "cast was rated" by Cronus's God within, and, therefore, he grew beyond his father's expectations and outgrew him. He had overstepped the rank of his father, and so he automatically robbed his father of his heavenly mind.

Cronus reigned in his father's place and cast his brothers – who were known as the Hundred Handed Ones and the Cyclops – into the land of Tartarus (we first notice that the word "tar" is repeated, where the relationship of our "truth ascends and releases", through the understanding of the Soul), which was where their father had already imprisoned them. Allow me to interpret the secret language regarding this sentence and explain that they had been robbed of their own mind, through sacrificing to their father; rather, they had lost control of their own power. Their testicles had not been removed in reality! Remember the codes of Enoch in regard to the story of Solomon's Temple?

Cronus then married Rhea ("releasing the heavenly 'EA'"), who was supposedly his sister. Let me explain that, throughout the mythical agenda, brothers and sisters do not actually form a relationship; this is merely the way that we have understood (or misunderstood) the language, because we had not yet evolved up into the unconscious mind. The correct interpretation is that Cronus began to educate himself, and, through his intellectual inheritance, his mind "married" – or came together through both hemispheres of his brain melding into one – which allowed his emotional mind to walk before his ego. He had walked up to the doorway of his unconscious mind. Through this deliverance, he could not allow any of his own children, who symbolically represent his future, to live.

Through understanding his Divine knowledge, he began to realize that he would eventually lose his inner strength to his children, as they would automatically rob him of his next thought. He would begin to lose his superiority, and they would gain from his strength and eventually overpower him. Remember the story of Herod, who declared himself a king and then tried to kill the firstborn son in every family?

The story moves on to inform us that Cronus, who was the father of Zeus, ate his own children. When his wife, Rhea, became pregnant with the child Zeus, she fled to the island of Crete ("creation"), where she hid in a cave (representing the womb) until it was time for the child's birth. This story is similar to the birthing of Jesus – or as the name Jesus was known in the first time, "He-Zeus". The child Zeus was left to be reared by the oceanid (sea nymph) Metis, which, when explained through the Metaphysical energy, is the Collective Consciousness. Thus, Zeus grew up to be free in the mind, knowing that he could reach his own maturity.

Let's look more closely at the word "oceanid". The word "oceanus" represents the consciousness – or the optical illusion, which becomes the mirage; that never-ending sea in the distance. The more you travel, the more you realize that it stays the same distance ahead of you. It is always there. It is only when you step outside your own boundaries – or the restrictions that you have placed around yourself for your own protection – that the mirage seems to come closer. The word "id" represents the "intelligence of your desire to release your inner kingdoms through opening your heart to self".

So the word "oceanid" is represented as a "lake". It is the creation of your consciousness. The word "Metis", I will explain in two levels. The first one is the explanation of the Latin word "meta", which is explained thus: "a pillar at each end of the field; a turning point, a goal that we reach and accomplish". The letters "is" represent the "intelligence of the Soul", and also the seals of "EL".

We bring all this together to explain that the "Metis" is an accomplishment that we have succeeded in attaining through our truth reaching up into its highest point of intellect, which we know is the explanation of the Egyptian "Ma'at". Now we can also see how the Latin language was collected through the discovery of each learned one walking up his/her own ladder to discover the self; in other words, for each to reach the doorway into his/ her unconscious mind.

Now to continue on with the story! Rhea (who represents the "Rha" of "EA") returned to Cronus, presenting her husband with a stone wrapped in swaddling clothes, which he understood to be his new child, and he swallowed the stone. In other words, Cronus swallowed the thoughts of his own mind, and Zeus was saved.

Zeus grew up, and he came unto his father, forcing him to swallow a potion of truth (his own medicine). Cronus became ill and regurgitated all his other children, whom he had previously swallowed. (Amazing, isn't it? If this story out in today's society, there would be hell to pay! We have carried these stories within our consciousness for thousands of years, and yet we still do not fully understand the original messages!)

The family then gathered together again to liberate the Hundred Handed Ones and the Cyclops from their own imprisonment. Collectively, they declared war on Cronus, whose allies were the Titians (note the spelling, as opposed to the traditional "Titans"). This saga then became another series of stories known as "The Battle of the Titians", which, when interpreted is representing the war between the ego and the emotions the ego is submitting; in other words, the left brain is still trying to claim its own supremacy.

Again, we see the similarity to the stories of Jesus, where, for eighteen years, he went out searching for his light to become Jesus Christ. The camp of the Titians were gathered on Mount Othrys, which is denoted as the "mountain of the Oracle of truth" – or another understanding is that it is releasing the eye of Horus, as explained in the hieroglyphs in Egypt. Zeus occupied Mount Olympus, and because he was the one who lived through finding his inner strength, he became the first Olympian. We now begin to notice a change in the story, as the Hundred Handed Ones had evolved and became the Three Hundred Handed Ones (they had collected themselves through their three inner Gods birthing themselves) who hurled huge rocks at the Titians. We know that the rocks represent the mind, and so now we understand how the "Titians" had to grow up and accept their next step of intellectual growth. (Now I will explain the reason for the different spelling of the name of the "Titians" in this version of the story. Do you see the reference to the name of the Egyptian Queen "Nefer-titi", who was the nurturer?) Victory had regaled for the Gods of Olympus, and the newly selected Deity named Zeus, whose knowledge birthed another generation of Gods, became superior in his own nation, as he now represented all the elements of his DNA.

The story is told that the Cyclops gave Zeus the title "God of Lightning" and the symbol of the thunderbolt.

The God Cronus represents the area known to us today as the "crown of the head". He married Rhea, whose name was taken from the city of Rosetta; they finally delivered their last child, who was named Zeus – or, Xios, as the ancient city from which the name of Zeus derives. In Germany, when I heard one of my students pronounce "Zeus" – which is still pronounced in the ancient way of "Tzios" in German – I realized this, and the whole story connected.

Finally, we come to the story of the Cyclops – the "giants among men" – who could see from their inner eye, which awakens when we have completed the journey of enlightenment, where both brains have been brought into unison with one another.

Our next reference is to Patroclus, through the Greek myths of Achilles and the Trojan War, which is explained in the "Iliad" of Homer (the "heavenly oracle of the meer", i.e., ocean). Patroclus was Achilles's closest friend, and he begged Achilles to do something to stop the Trojans when they were about to burn the Greek ships out in the harbour at Troy. (These ships represent the embodiment of the personalities of self – or the tribe they all belonged to.) Achilles, who was known for his stubbornness, refused to budge, and so Patroclus (through the Metaphysical explanation, Achilles's "closest friend" represents his closest personality, which supported and stood beside him) put on the armour of Achilles, and he went out to do battle in his friend's place. The Trojans, who were led by Hector, retreated back to their own city, intimidated by Achilles, a warrior of great renown. Alas! The God Apollo informed Hector that it was not really Achilles, but his best friend, Patroclus, who stood in his place. As a result, Hector set out and killed Patroclus.

Another battle ensued over the killing of Patroclus, where Achilles went into battle to avenge Patroclus (gift of his closest personality), and again the Trojans fled. Thus, the battle came down to a one-on-one confrontation between Hector and Achilles, who met at the Scaean Gates. (This sacred place is the forehead, where the two minds vie for supremacy, and a fortuitous agreement must come to order; another explanation is the machine used in the medical world to "scan" the human body. Through the Metaphysical, it is the place where your dreams are returned to you.) Hector was killed, and Achilles attached the corpse behind his chariot, dragging it around the city walls of Troy. After that, he went to attend the funeral of his best friend. The body of Patroclus was placed on a burning raft that the Greeks released out into the ocean. The burning raft represents the resurrection of the Soul; this is where we are released from the earth in order to be born again. (The Metaphysical story of Achilles is explained in another chapter of this book.)

Please take a break here and drink a glass of water, which will help you release some of the tension that the ego commits you to when it receives a rebound of information.

I will continue on to give you a brief Metaphysical explanation regarding the story of Delphi, who was the wife of Apollo for 1,000 years. She claimed to live in the "navel of the world" (which the Greeks called the omphalos) – or, through the codes, the "AN" (the educated one). Zeus let four eagles fly from each corner of the earth, and when they met in the centre and crossed over one another, he called the area "the Delphi", which means "the Divine everlasting power of heavenly intelligence". Again, we see the four directions coming together, as explained in Isaiah 43:5–6, "Fear not: for I am with thee: I will bring thy seed from the east, and gather thee from the west; I will say to the north, give up; and to the south, keep not back: bring my sons from far; and my daughters from the ends of the earth." Now we understand that the sons represent the power of the next thought, and the daughters represent the emotions we need to balance ourselves. Another Greek name that I find very interesting is the ancient city of Trisonea ("Tri-son-ea"), which is explained through the codes as the "three sons of 'EA'". Do you see how those three sons are again representing the three Gods ("EL", "AN", "EA")?

The city of Paxi is the Latin name which represents the "power of the inner light" – or the serenity one finds within. The Corinth Canal is the "Core of Inte". "Inte" is also the name of God, through both the Egyptian and Mayan languages. (Is this where we grasped the name "Int-el" for our inner computer?)

Ithica (usually spelt "Ithaca") is the famed island, supposedly the home of Odysseus ("ode to Zeus"), which is also similar to the stories of Jesus that concurrently offer the same explanation. In the ancient language, "It-ic-kha" denotes as "my intellect is my truth, through the intelligence of the creation of knowing my heavenly ascension". The word changed when the Romans began to understand the codes of the Greek legends and included this name into the Latin vocabulary. The name "Itaka" was taken by the Romans, and we now refer to them as "It-EL-EA'AN's" – or Italians.

I felt excited when I came to realize that I was visiting so many disciplines – the Biblical Resonances, Medical Sciences, Philosophy, and Astronomy – all of which decoded the same exact meanings at the exact same time! Allow me to initiate you into our history, where we are able to understand how these names came into being. We journey back through to the Egyptian testimonials, into the area known as Lower Egypt.

This expression is represented as the God P'tah in Egypt, which is – known through symbolism as the dove; through the Bible, this is known as Peter – hence, the stained-glass window of the white dove in St Peter's Basilica in Rome.

Digressing from Greece for a moment, I will give you another name to recognize: the city of "Es-Pha-AN" "through the eternal Soul, my power heavenly ascends as God". The country of Iran, through the Metaphysical codes, is known as "UR-AN", which is explained to us as "you understanding and releasing" – or "you're 'AN'". Hence, throughout the Arabic kingdoms, this place was known as the "City of Education", where all the scholars congregated.

The light that comes from the name of a city is what draws humanity to that place, through the codes of the name – or "nome". This where a citadel is placed as an "icon" – or a "glyph of light" for all to view. Through the language of the unconscious mind, you will find that every language on the planet hears the same story, no matter how they speak or where they live. We are all one!

Notes:

CHAPTER TWENTY TWO

Travelling Along The Old Silk Road

I took a large group of students to Turkey a couple of years ago, and we spent three wonderful weeks travelling along the old Silk Road, and, from there, on to the trails of old Mesopotamia, which our guide referred to as the "Land of the Sumer of Ea". We had a wonderful Turkish guide who introduced us to his family and made us feel welcome. He held quite an exalted position in his village, and he revered his forefathers' stories, which he wanted to share with us. His family had lived in the same area for more than 860 years, and they still had the records for hundreds of these years. He had never moved from the area, so his whole existence was right there. He took us across his land in his old bus, village by village. He came from way, way back in time. His stories were not surmised; they were handed down from father to son, and, through his not venturing out to explore beyond his horizons, he still held the codes of the original understanding of what was said. He was invaluable to me regarding the body language and the biblical hierarchy. He knew them all, and I hope, in the future, to make you aware of all of them.

In one of the villages up in the mountains, we met the village Elder, who had fourteen daughters; from four years of age, each of them had all been trained to become a carpet weaver. They went into the weaving shed, sat beside a female Elder, and learned the art of weaving the rugs patterned to explain the mythical storytelling; these small children first learned the mathematics of tying many different styles of the knots on the end of the large carpets. The children's little fingers were so nimble! They sat up there beside their bigger sisters and aunties, and they listened to the different stories explaining the difference in the geometric patterns that they would learn to weave. In the main weaving shed of more than forty women, so much peace and harmony abounded! We listened to the stories of the older members of the family, and then they sang their ancient songs to while away the hours. They still conversed in the ancient Aramaic language, and their father was a relative of our guide. We went over to his house for tea, where all the women made us feel very welcome. There was much handshaking and hugs and smiles and tears as we tasted their succulent cuisine. Then came the recipe swapping; which explained everything in hand measurements, with pinches of this and that spice.

The Elder of the village wanted to show me something, so he asked me to follow him outside. Next thing I knew, I was down on all fours, crawling under the house and into his chicken coop, which was down amongst the foundations. That is where he showed me some old Sumerian rock carvings that had been there since his forefathers had built the house all those generations before. The walls were more than 60 centimetres thick, and the foundations of the house were built into solid rock. They had no worries regarding it falling down! They had chipped away at the base rock to form these elongated grooves, and then they had placed huge slabs of rock inside them. There were gaps between these large slabs and the rock, and I asked him, "Aren't you worried about the movement of the house through these gaps?" He replied, "No! When the mountains move, our home moves with them, and this always keeps my home steadied. My home is as solid as the rock. On a windy night we are all rocked to sleep." Now why didn't I think of that? So simple! When the top of the house became weather-worn from the strong winds that blew across the valley, they just replaced the top section of the house.

We entered deep into the Mesopotamian evolution and the meeting grounds of the ancient ones who handed down "the stories of the day before", as my guide explained time to me. I loved their way of speaking. I could hear my own Aboriginal language coming through the old ways of their communication; even the pronunciations sounded the same. We saw the magnificent giant heads of the Gods that had been carved long ago, set to look out and defend the people. They were metres high; some of them had fallen over through the movement of the sand, and some were still buried – and yet, they were still doing what they were placed there to do. They were the foundations representing their people's personalities, and they were revered as Gods who would watch over the people and help them maintain the strength to go on.

The Mesopotamian story is similar to the stone heads on Easter Island, where some of the heads face out over the land towards the waters – which are representing the personalities of the mind looking towards the consciousness, searching for their answers from the Divine. To this day, many of these statues still have not been finished. These statues are representing our personalities that are in a transitional period – that is, in the process of converting up into the One God. And then there were other statues that face over the land and have their backs to the water. They represent the "protectors" – or the "overlords" – of the consciousness, who watch over the people as they convert their mind up into the Metaphysical – or Spiritual – resonance.

My guide knew the stories of all the Gods and what they had brought from heaven to earth. I must pause to give thanks to those who guided us during this wonderful journey in Turkey. Thank you, my precious Khadea, for all your stories. "Kha-Di-EA" means "the knowledge of the Divine worth of God". My thanks also go to my wonderful Mehmet for your unfailing interpretation during my seminars, explaining to the Turkish people my journey of the "Language of the Soul". I could have sat there for years just listening to your stories regarding the glories of your past.

Your land speaks its own mask to you, its own Collective Consciousness. You are here to evolve and become your own myth; that is the journey of the Soul, the Metaphysical Collective Consciousness. Remember that these ancient lands still hold the keys that we are searching for, that will remind us how we bring the mosaic of man together.

Notes:

CHAPTER TWENTY THREE

Electromagnetic Energy Fields Coincide Throughout The Universes

The electromagnetic energy fields coincide throughout the Universes, and they vibrate to an eclectic field of orbital correlation. Every mountain range on this planet is created through the mathematics of a star system of a similar equation of transmissible energy. It is amazing that the numerology that surrounds us, is also embedded in our genes, where each section composes its inner sound. This sound is alphabetically echoed and is transferred throughout the wholeness as it harmonizes and rebalances each layer of consciousness.

Every hill, valley, and river is also set through eclectic energies which are drawn from the Laws of the Universe; they coincide with an imperative movement of secular energy. As the star systems rotate, so, too, does the earth move through the same sequences? This transference cohabitates and holds an autonomic construction of formulized fusion. As it is above, so it is below.

I do know that my life force has been a help to the gravitational force fields of this planet; it is something I have always known. I don't know what it is that I've known; I have just always known. My father explained to me as a child that we each are just as important as everyone else and we each have our own role to fulfil.

Have you ever realized that your role is an important factor to keep the alphabet and numbers correlating in their correct order? Play your role, as you know it to be; not what others expect of you. Remember that this covenant is one that we sacredly make through birthing into our tribe; it carries us forward in order for us to realize that, if we stay nonchalant with our thoughts, our sacredness will always surround us, even as we venture out into greener pastures.

CHAPTER TWENTY FOUR

My Journey

As a child, I could never stand crowds of people around me. I had difficulties breathing freely within the mass of other people's energy; it choked me, so my parents deliberately kept me isolated.

When I was three years old, my parents took me to the local show that was held in our bush town once a year. Show time was when we of the Outback came alive. Everyone caught up with what everyone else had been doing since we'd last met, and smiles were abundant all around. We all had new outfits to wear for this major yearly event, and the women had new hats of all shapes and sizes. The men could compare how many bags to the acre they were hoping they could harvest through the forthcoming wheat season. They were subconsciously relating to their friends the amount of money that the wheat cheque had the possibility of becoming, if the weather stayed fine. It was a time to share; where differences with, and indifferences towards, one another were all on hold.

The women were either exchanging recipes or medical assumptions, and their little notebooks and pencils came out as they engaged one another in conversation. I once asked my father why the men wore such large hats, and he explained to me that the bigger the brim on the hat, the bigger the overdraught the man had with his bank! Whilst hiding under the brim of his hat, he could also keep hiding from himself.

Back to the show when I was three. On that day, as we walked among such a large crowd, I became dizzy from so many people continuously walking past me, and I fainted. My father picked me up, dusted me down, and carried me. He was wiping the dirt off my face with his handkerchief when a woman came up and tapped him on the arm. "Look after that little one; she has a very important job to do in the future," she said. My father had never seen this woman before in his life, but he proudly said, "Yes, she is my daughter; and so, to me, she is very important!" "No, sir, you don't understand," the woman said. "She is the one that Edgar Cayce spoke about. She will reveal the secrets."

My father had never heard of this name before, and so had not read any of Edgar Cayce's works, but he made it a point to do so. He went to the local library in town and ordered the books; when they arrived at our library from the city, my father read them – he never forgot what that woman said to him that day at the show. He kept me under a tight rein, and he always said that he understood the "nonsense" I was babbling about. He was a gentle man who always found the time to listen. My father shared all this information with me on the last day we spent together; he was taken to hospital the next morning, and he died three days later.

He was an amazing father and the best teacher any child could ask for; by the time I was five years old, my father was teaching me about the star systems. I could not remember the names, although I could find them simply by the symbol that they formed in the sky. Have you ever stood under the stars in the Australian Outback? They look very large and magnificently bright, and they seem to hang just above your head. I had a large window in my bedroom, and I loved watching the stars turn around. They were there one minute and gone the next, and a new set was preparing itself for me to view. I seemed to be able to see through the stars – through my eyes, they were layer upon layer, going deep into space. My mind's eye had always been working on my behalf, and I found out later that I was viewing everything through its own perspective, which was reflecting its image back to me in 3D.

For my ninth birthday, I received from my father a series of sepia photos of the burial chamber of the Pharaoh Tutankhamen ("Tut-Ankh-Amon"); my father had received these photos as a gift years before, and he was passing them on to me. I loved these photos, and I looked at them often throughout my life. I can still remember the words he would say whenever I became fearful as a child: "Fear not, my little girl; remember that your faith is always answered." For that same birthday, my grandmother gave me a box of old pen nibs that she had been carrying around for more than sixty years. She told me to make pens from the grandest feathers I could find, and then use those pens to write down my thoughts, because they would become my stories. Well, it is nigh on sixty years later, and you are now reading them! It is only at the age I am now that I can see the significance of the gifts that I had been given throughout my life. I am living my program that my previous generations had prepared for me.

I had a deep-seated dream to go and see the Pyramids, and I knew that they were here for all mankind, not just for the Egyptians. God placed everything in exactly the right place; there has never been a mistake, and there never will be. If it cannot fathom its own reality, it cannot construct itself. That is a natural assumption that comes through our alphabet as we speak to create these Universal laws, and it is how we balance our numerology which we refer to as mathematics – or "Ma'at-He-Ma'at-ic's" – working through the Collective Mind.

We are a Collective of "Soul energy"; it makes no difference what land you belong to or what language you speak. Everything we receive on this planet is here in deference to one another, to show us how this planet we call home shall take its place among the Universes. It is this Soul energy that is the overriding factor of why we are here. We have come so far as to our understanding of our intellectual awakening, and our technology is so superior to that of 100 years ago. We are so fortunate to have everything at our fingertips to support us in our industrial relationships with one another; that makes our life so much easier. And the wonder of the computer has become our inner eye opener, where we can travel the planet and search for the answers to our thoughts through the tips of our fingers. Now that is our alphabet and numerology explaining their earnings to broadcast their rights of passage!

CHAPTER TWENTY FIVE

Returning Home To Babylon

Let me divulge in a story of something that happened to me in Egypt. I had been staying with my friend, who is a sheik ("sha-ik" or "cha-ic"), a title that he had just received through the death of his father, passed down to him through his tribal inheritance. We were talking about the work his father had done to support the many thousands he was responsible for; I was explaining to him how the next generation must fill the previous generation's shoes to keep their entitlement continuing. Those shoes have to fit comfortably in order for the next wearer to walk in an upright position. The next generation must grow up and accept extra responsibilities in order for the inheritance to work for them as it did for their father.

My friend's feet were larger than his father's, so he had to realize that his potentialities could climb much higher; he could take his inheritance and reach up to accomplish much greater heights. We were interrupted from our morning talk, as a group of his advisors entered the room to confer with him, and so he excused himself. I moved my chair further back, as he did not want me to leave the room. They spoke in Arabic, so I began assessing through myself what we had already discussed so that I could add to our conversation when we began again.

As their conversation came closer to me, I felt my mind lifting up into the silence. My heart began to pound and jump up beneath my tongue as I heard their language being spoken to me in Old English. I became very excited at this revelation and began to pay more attention. The etheric layers created through their talking had found a compatible resonance within me, and I realized that I was returning home to Babylon. I explained this to my friend when he had finished with his conference, and, when I could repeat what they had spoken in Arabic, which I do not speak, my friend was as amazed as I was. Once again, it confirmed for me that this was the alphabet at work as to how it sifted each letter through each language to promote itself for the next educated step to inherit. English is the last language to birth and it has been created letter by letter from the others. There is only one language, which has been carried by the wind to the four corners of the globe where we can find the peace within our self in order for us to be able to hear it!

My grandmother had this wonderful little picture that I had grown up seeing, and I loved this picture all my life. Placed in the vestibule as you walked into the house, it was an old Arabic proverb: "I had no shoes and complained, until I met a man who had no feet."

Notes:

CHAPTER TWENTY SIX

Numerology

We move on to the Divinity of Numbers, which collects through the Sacred Alphabet, working through the same etheric levels and then beginning to facet a coherent behaviour, where it multiplies and releases each number which has been autonomically registered up into the unconscious mind. It is through the acceptance of numbers that we are introduced up into the Sacred Geometry, which is a language of our higher education between our self and God. It creates a structure, where we can conform and become all things through using the strength of our numbers, one digit at a time. Each number is created through a resonance that empowers itself, alerting the conscious, subconscious, and unconscious minds – all of which multiplies through this additional intellect, and we learn to harmonize our thoughts with our self and with one another. Each number creates its applicability through the levels of intellectual conversation that we have with one another. When your mind becomes balanced with your aura, the correct number is then transformed through your mind. Maybe through this explanation you can see how you had to birth on that very special day. The numbers of your birthday add up to a language of the responsibility you have the opportunity to uphold on behalf of your tribal law. They are tools that work with the self and through the unconscious mind.

This is how we are beginning to realize the stories of our past. These mythical stories explain to us why it is written that Noah lived for 950 years. The newer versions of the Bible changed this hidden coded language before humanity came to understand the unconscious recognition of the original story. As a result, it now sounds like a different story, as, through the old ways, the numerology was explaining a code of recognition as to how both hemispheres of the brain evolve up into the unconscious mind. These original numbers are carrying the story through an inner vibration, which is autonomically collecting throughout our nervous system and adding to the personification of self. It connects us up into the unconscious energy, and, when we understand this language, we have the ability to relate to a more detailed account of our thoughts. In other words, our intelligence reinvests in itself so that our knowledge can expand and become more pronounced.

Let me explain it this way: Noah, through these three numbers of his age (950) is also alerting us to the fact that he had to die to his past ways so that he could now "know all of himself through his advancement", which is the code to number nine (9); this gave him the "freedom of his mind", which is the number five (5); to "accept the information that is implanted in his Soul", which is the number zero (0). Now allow me to bring these three numbers together in this sentence: "Through knowing myself, I have finished with my past, which creates my freedom to understand my Soul." Yes, it sounds quite difficult to begin with, but it does not take too long before you swing into the relationship of this embedded language that is impregnated in your genes.

All numbers are powerful, when you fully understand the value of the thought that they must work with. They work in the negative, as well as the positive, and the Laws of the Universe present them to you for a reason – or a resonance – in order for you to work through them and bring your thoughts up into a balance that is part of the Collective. Remember that the conscious mind works in single digits, and the responsibility is yours to accept, emotionally, how you collate to bring those numbers together. The totality of the answer presented to you will depend on how the sonar, which you symbolically create, registers your mathematics back to you as to what you have already achieved; this is delivered back to you in its pure truth. We cannot lie with numbers.

Maybe now you can understand how the employees of major corporations who think that they can "help themselves" to reap the benefits of money that is not theirs in the first place always get caught in the long run. You cannot keep lying to the Collective; it is much stronger than you are. Karma will always be returned to you, especially when you are over controlling someone else's attention. Stock markets crash, banking industries falter, etc.; always, this is the result of our action spiralling ever higher. Other people have invested in this or that company in order to reap their own rewards, but usually not to keep the company functioning on its own merits. Remember, the ultimate aim of the language of the unconscious energy always finalizes everything we think and do in numbers. If the results of your action do not strike you, those close to you in the next generations (i.e., your children, grandchildren, and so on) will certainly inherit your lies. This is the ultimate deliverance to the mathematics of our mind.

It does not matter how many digits you wish to use; they must be sounded out one at a time, in the beginning, in order for you to learn this higher code of conscription. Let us take, for example, one of the most powerful numbers: 333. We do not group the number as "three hundred thirty three"; instead, we repeat the singular sound – "three, three, three". We know that the number three (3) represents the Mind of God, so when we group these three numbers together, the result becomes the "mind's mind". Through saying this, we release an understanding that the mind must measure the mind, and so the competition is on. This is in relationship to left-brain thinking.

Now allow me give you a positive, which is accepted as the responsibility of the right brain's intuitiveness, and say that "the mind mirrors the mind". This equation is so much more positive, and it is what our pituitary gland relies upon: $3 + 3 + 3 = 9$. The number nine (9) is the last of the single digits; when decoded, it equates to the symbol of death. We are talking about the Noah – or the "Knower of ways" – here; it is an ending of one world in order for us to die to our old ways so that we can be free to advance into the next one.

We begin to bring together those "three threes" (333) that have eclectically and divinely collected through the religious experience of self. When we view the symbol of the "OM", you will see that the Sanskrit character looks like the number three (3). Symbolically, this explains to us that our understanding, acceptance, and action become one, and this union must equalize each hemisphere of the brain into "one-ness". Now we can understand how the number nine (9) is an ending that allows the step up into the next world to present itself to us so that we can go on. When I am conversing with a client, my mind communicates back to me in numerical form; I pay attention to the numbers that I receive in my vision worlds, which give me a complete sentence. I had to learn to tune in to my heartbeat, which explains to me the equation that I need to know in order to determine whether the numbers are relayed in a collective or singular pattern.

For instance, if the numbers that release for me are 3-27-84, those three numbers inform me that the person I am speaking to, who has a terminal dis-ease, also has the opportunity to repair his/her thinking and correct the overload of his/her own energy. In other words, there is no permanent damage to the mind and body; anyone can change and correct his/her thinking, if he/she so desires, in order for the body to autonomically repair itself. I am being given the information that it is not too late – this person has a second chance to reinvest in the self. He/she has been caught up into that realm of intellect in order for one of the personalities to embellish its own behaviour. It is like a tug of war in the family as to who will reign supreme. The sentence that equates to the numbers 3-27-84 is: "Through the mind, he/she must accept the understanding of the relationship to his/ her emotional teachings; he/she must learn to harmonize the mind in order to balance the temple – or inner self".

From those numbers, I know where that person's shortfalls are, and that shows me how to transcribe what I have received numerically into a sentence that will explain it to him/her. This information has helped my psychiatry students more clearly understand the worlds of mentally challenged, who are still trapped in their own darkness, intellectually. Their fear has suppressed them, locking them into obstinate behaviour.

It is time for us all to drink a large glass of water, to cleanse and relax, so that we may resound into our eternalness.

The next number is the number ten (10). When we refer to this number, we have automatically opened up into the subconscious mind, which is the wisdom of the right brain. This explains to you the resonance known as "Akhenaton", who was supposedly the tenth Pharaoh in Egypt. Remember that the first nine numbers are in single digits. So, when we reach up to the number ten (10), we are bringing in the zero (0) to repeat ourselves again. This time, we are including the right brain, as well as the left. This is where the word "dichotomy" is collected, and we become much more responsible for everything we say and do. We are awakening and connecting to the inner truth.

Through my eyes, when I had fully understood the mathematics of this beautiful being of light that we have named Akhenaton, I could understand what he was representing through his own purification of his intelligence; I definitely wanted to learn more. He was both male and female (or was it pronounced "phi-male" at that time?) This explains his body shape that is recorded in his statues. He was announcing to us the next evolutionary step that humanity can step up into, which is the Metaphysical journey of enlightenment. And remember that the word "Metaphysics" is reminding us of the matter of physics; explaining how matter evolved into becoming pure. Through my eyes, he represents the first person in history who honoured himself. Now do you begin to understand the writing on the walls? Does this explain the words "Meni meni tekal u pha sin", which is denotes as, "the days of thy kingdom are numbered"?

The stories of Egypt were recorded for all humanity to earn. They are the stories of our availability to enter up into the next dimension of humanity's intellect; it is where we take the time to unravel the bandages that we have wrapped around us, which represent our inherited fear. The ego must grow up to be prepared for the afterlife. Never mind about dropping dead! This next world is the world of non-attachment and non-judgement. It is the world of obtaining the freedom of self.

The Sacred Numerology assists us, and we find that it rearranges our thinking and keeps our mind's pantry cupboard sorted out. We must know what is on our shelves; we don't just reach in and grab any bottle of thought. And this pantry of thoughts is also the bank that holds our memories. We must learn to take our time to listen to ourselves in order to be able to see what we are capable of creating – before the scene collects itself on our behalf.

Let me go into this again and refresh your mind. There is the first-dimensional mind of the God "EL", through the myth, and this area is the beginning of our Metaphysical journey. We are all connected through this intelligence, whether you are aware of it or not! It is the first doorway into our mythical experiences, where we learn to understand our true self, which helps to unravel our inner freedom. Remember that the word "mythology" is denoted as "my theology" – or "my way of life". Our mythology is a significant omen that releases back to us on an unconscious level in order to create, on our behalf, an added responsibility as to how we can rearrange our thinking to reap those extra benefits due to us because we have earned them. There is something inside all of us that pertains to knowing we are entitled to more, and, when we understand these events through Numerology, we can use these added tools to supplement our understanding.

Now we have the confidence to create our dreams, which is arranged metaphysically on our behalf, through the symbolic language of numerology. Its compliance with us is controlled through our sexuality, which, of course, is the creation of our ego. The results of this section of the body fortifies the left hemisphere of the brain, which is our logic self. This is the section of our lower body; from our hips, it sways up to the navel area. Once we have come to terms with this section of our body and have realized our past inheritance, the first step of our freedom arrives to assist and guide us up into the next world of intellect.

We then move up into the second-dimensional mind of the God "AN", where we begin to accept our self through the responsibility of our thinking, which means to answer on behalf of our thoughts, as this offers us a greater potentiality to release and use our possibilities. The middle kingdom of "AN" frees us from our old restrictions, and we then have the strength to accept our thoughts much more positively, as a result of releasing what we had previously allowed to control us. Does this mean that sex is no longer of any importance? No, of course not. It means that all this is a library of information that we now understand about ourselves, as a result of having released the bound-up fear delivered to us through our own tribal creation.

This area is our educational system; it begins at the navel, where the first dimensional area ends, and it encompasses stomach and heart area. As our university begins to unite our verse, we become balanced and more harmonized through gathering our personalities together. It is through the beat of our heart, where the energy spirals throughout the heartbeat, for the Fibonacci to collect and create itself. Again, we have reached up to our next mathematical measurement through attaining and balancing our mind, which reaches up to prepare us to walk into the ethereal layer of our intellect. You have heard it all before.

The final step is approaching, where we move up into the third dimension, through the gathering of the two previous Gods who have learned to meld and blend together; this is the doorway to the God "EA". Once we have understood how our intelligence is releasing, we move into the upper hierarchy of knowing that our intelligence is our light, and we are able to accept the gift of being advanced holographically – this is where we can enter up into the unconscious mind. I am explaining how the left brain or ego is reaching its zenith through the single digits.

When we bring in the number ten (10), we must begin again, continuing up the next rung of the ladder; we step up, and this is where the subconscious mind – or the right hemisphere of the brain – begins to mirror, support, and strengthen us, adding to our Numerology. Do you begin to see how each brain reaches its peak of perfection, after which it is autonomously collected to be measured up through and into the unconscious mind, where the mathematics must complete itself? It is a poignant time with self, as it gives you a chance to explore these myths that have been released through your previous inheritance and passed on for you to endure. There are hundreds of thousands of mythical stories that have been explained in all languages, over thousands of years; when you have time, please feel free to read a few of them, and you will understand more clearly much of what I am now reminding you to recall. Please remember that your personalities are these recorded stories that have been written and passed on; you are participating in and living every one of them at every moment – and especially in the moments when you are ready to release your next thought.

We are beginning to understand more clearly the Arabic translation of the word "Himalaya" – or "Hi-Ma'Allah-EA" or, through to the Germanic language, the "Himmel-of–Aya". The German word "Himmel" interprets as the "heaven of 'EA'". We are watching Babylon at work here, and we find that it is representing the land above the clouds, which symbolically represents the unconscious mind. The clouds represent the fear that releases through your DNA in order for you to overcome it. This is also the totem pole throughout the Eastern philosophies. Maybe now you can understand my previous explanations about the mist that collects on the earth, which symbolically represents your future inheritance.

Allow me to refresh your mind in regard to the two hemispheres of the brains: The left brain is through the God "EL" (everlasting life), and the right brain is through the God "AN" (ascending and nourishing) We are beginning to see how the mathematics of each myth collected, and how many stories of the Gods were written for us through the ancient language. All of those Gods had to evolve to become one. This temple energy is cohabitated as the judicial system of the mind, which begins to collect through the glands around the neck area, travelling up through and around our ears, and then up into the temple area in front of the ears. This is where we are unconsciously preparing the sacredness that we give to self – that is, as to how our own sonic sound reaches out and releases into the Collective of all. Slowly, we are reaching an understanding of these laws through the Collective Inheritance that we have all been born with. This is the doorway to us tuning in to our sonic sound. Sonar is a mathematical device that man has created in order to detect objects through the reflection of sound waves underwater. Sonar is represented the same way in the human body; it begins in the mastoid area behind our ears, where we hear a thought, and, through the reflection of our sound waves, each thought is then transferred to our middle ear, which transfers the message to the brain.

CHAPTER TWENTY SEVEN

The Shamanic Inheritance Of Numbers And Their Meanings

Allow me to initiate you into explaining the Shamanic Inheritance of numbers and their meanings.

1. I Am.

2. My Relationship; comes through acknowledging myself.

3. My Mind; is everything I am.

4. My Temple; my inner self; my education into discovering my darkness and my light.

5. My Freedom; I earn through the changes I have made to my self.

6. My Mastering; the gathering of one's self to master the understanding of all thought. Our ego loses its control over us when we accept the responsibility for every thought that we think. Can you see how 666 became the mark of the beast? It is not negative; it is a powerful number which informs us of the responsibility we have to live up to in order to know our own mind.

7. My Communication; it is our intuition; it belongs to our teacher within. It produces our light, which we have labelled our Christ consciousness. This number is also in relationship to the knowledge of the angelic realms.

8. My Balance and Harmony; this is the sign of infinity; where everything is available and waiting for you.

9. My Death; to my old ways, through the education of my understanding and knowing all.

0. My Soul; my Alpha and Omega.

When the numbers become double digits, we relate to the above and bring them together.

10. I Am my Soul.

11. I Am as I Am.

12. I Am my Relationship.

And so on, throughout the numbers. Thus, we are affirming and collecting our intellect with each digit.

When the numbers vibrate into the twenties, it is through the connection to the number two (2), which represents the relationship we can attain through self. When we reach up to the thirties, we are opening up into the mind of self; we are embellishing ourselves to our mind. The forties are much higher, and they begin to collect up into the temple of self. This is where we never try to repeat our mistakes. Both brains are realizing their intelligence, and this is where we are being tested through the consciousness to abstain from thinking in a negative way. We are beginning to enter up into the unconscious recognition of our mind. The fifties are, through the changes of the old ways, where we are able to release to earn the freedom of self. The sixties are, through the gathering of self, where we begin to familiarize and master self. The seventies are the teachings of self, where we have the ability to unconsciously reflect our intellectual earnings out in order to teach others. The eighties are the harmonizing of self with the infinite, where we begin to prosper. The nineties are the belief of knowing self, where we have the ability to move into the next thought and/or attract ourselves up into the next world.

Each step of your intelligence that you awaken from its long, deep sleep advances outside your own reflection, where others are alerted to your energy, and it is also where you become aware of them, before they see you. They are waiting for you to move into their psyche, as they know that you can help them answer their questions. Once they learn to understand themselves, they then move into yours. The world is full of beauty and grace, isn't it? We are always in the right place at the right moment. When I was collaborating with all of this ultra mathematics during my training, my heart ached so much at the wonderment of how these Universal Laws are always permanently working on our behalf. This gave me so much more confidence, and it opened my heart up to where I could understand how to release myself into the arms of the creator of all things.

When we have three repetitions of the number one (i.e., 111), we are starting to collect the mind together. We begin here by looking at the number one (1), which is "I am", and, as there are three repetitions, we realize that this denotes as, "I am my mind". The "I am" is being reminded of your awakening, and now you must make an important decision to trust yourself more and move forward into the relationship of self – that is, you must not keep on thinking that your mind is in charge of you.

Let me briefly explain the number 1,000,000; there are two ways of explaining these digits. From the left brain, we would respond to "I am forming a relationship to my Soul mind", and the right brain would read them as "I am mastering my Soul". The left brain is slower at comprehending each digit; whereas, the right brain is multifaceted. We are able to comprehend how the right brain is presenting a stronger belief in what we have already accomplished and attained.

These numbers have begun to collect and multiply on a subconscious level, and, when you become aware of the growth of your intellectual achievements, each number begins to appear before your eyes; this is where you are autonomically opening up your inner vision. Your intelligence seems to be climbing up your inner ladder of success as your DNA unravels through accepting its own strength. Other people who are familiar with you notice these changes; they begin to realize how assertive you are feeling towards yourself.

It takes time for the body to adjust to this new way of thinking, as you are being pushed out of your old safety harness. It is a much higher intellectual code of you understanding just what your capabilities are able to accomplish on your behalf. You are communicating through to your master system, which is opening up a doorway into your unconscious mind. You are automatically collecting your own self-worth.

How many of you have a repetition of the same number on your number plate, phone number, or bank account? One lady, who read out her bank account numbers during a seminar where I was explaining the Sacred Numerology, came to the realization that the only winner was the bank! She changed her bank and her account number, and she has never looked back. Her friend who sat next to her had the same bank, but she was of a different personality, and so her account numbers worked well for her, and she had no need to change. It all depends on which personality of self you allow to rule.

Notes:

CHAPTER TWENTY EIGHT

How We Rely On Numbers To Read The Hidden Language

The next step is to introduce you further into the worlds of Shamanism – that is, the way in which we rely on numbers to read the hidden language of how the Collective is reimbursing our truth back to us. This is also your introduction into the language of the body. We begin with the hidden language of God, who lives in your consciousness and vibrates your thoughts up into the Collective Consciousness; this is where and how the mathematics began to equate telepathically with your Soul.

The more stimulated your thoughts become, the more opportunities you will be able to use to your benefit. Do you see how I am bringing both the languages of religion and science together? Remember, your ego needs religion, and your emotions need science; you must have both in order for you to benefit and advance the left and right hemispheres of the brain up into their temple inheritance.

Whatever thought you have in your mind is automatically being reflected back to you instantly; this happens as soon as you allow your mind to think. The world is your mirror, and it is always assessing your thinking. It sounds ridiculous, doesn't it? Every thought you think to form a continuance of your energy creates a sentence, which, in turn, is reflected back to you. It begins from the first sentence that you hear on the TV when you turn it on. Spilling your drink, dropping a cup, slipping on the floor, cutting your finger, etc. – all these are part of the process. Remember, there is never a mistake! Every consequence in your life is through the results of your thinking; all of it mirrors back to you, every moment of every day. When you are out walking, the bird in the sky, or the dog or cat walking across your path, is a mirror image of your thought in that moment. If you see or hear car tires screeching around a corner, and the brakes slammed on; if a fire engine races by, or an ambulance siren screams in the distance – please start to take notice of what is surrounding you.

If a car horn sounds once when you are out walking, you must immediately bring your thought back to the self. This single sound means that you need to pay attention to your thoughts, as they are running away from you; you're losing control! That horn is a warning, so watch the thought you are having in that moment. If the car horn sounds twice, it means that you must come back into yourself and rebalance your mind; you need to come back and form a relationship with these thoughts of the moment. If it sounds three times, it means pay attention to the whole experience of your thinking. When we hear the same sound four times, it means that it is a sign of destruction to a temple thought, so eradicate your thoughts immediately and begin again.

If you notice a bird in the sky, it reminds you to think from an angelic perspective; please fly higher with your thoughts of that moment. Remind yourself that you should use it in the singular; that thought should only be used for the self. That angel with wings is saying to you, "Come on, move up and fly higher!" Two birds relate to the relationship of your thoughts; in other words, start to bring your thoughts into the Collective Mind. Three birds relate to your mind; start to improve your thinking, etc. If you hear a dog bark, it means that you are dwelling in the past with your thinking; the animal mind relates to our ancient past. Count the number of barks, and then refer to the list above. Dogs represent the emotion of loyalty, so that dog is reminding you to be loyal to your thinking. Stop wasting your time with miscellaneous thinking!

I would like to explain to you how the Collective is answering your thoughts, whether it is a fly buzzing around you, a beetle walking on the ground, a leaf falling from a tree, and so on. Humankind has evolved from the first species to inherit the earth. They have been created through one of them believing in themselves. As each species created the next generation, we all inherited. Man is the last to evolve, and our brain has been created through every other species earning their own emotional inheritance. It has had to be this way; this is God at work. The whole planet is a thought that learned to believe in itself. Learn how we are able to see how the human brain invested in itself! Where does your animal live in your body, and what emotion does it represent in you? Where does your bird tribe live in you? Where in you is the fish of the ocean? Why have the eternal species invented the insect world?

Listen to the Shamanic symbolism of evolution. Listen as I explain how we learned to stand upright: The soles of our feet were energized through things that lived under the ground; we became gravitized, and then we became the grass and the trees up to our ankles. They all stood still, and the only way they could move was through their seeds being carried by the energy of the wind. From our ankles, we began to evolve as the animal has supported itself, up to our knees. We refer to this section of our body as our ancient past. From the knees, we began to inherit the educated mind of all of these species, which travelled up to our navel. All of this section represents our ego, and it is under the auspicious command of our left brain. From the navel, we are introduced to the bird tribes, where we learn to educate ourselves and reach up towards our heart, and you have already read what this section means – it is where we learn to open our heart to create our own wings; where, symbolically, we can learn to soar in the mind. Do you remember the myth of Zeus and the four eagles that supposedly crossed the centre of the earth, at the place known as the Temple of Delphi?

From here we are introduced into the oceanic species of the fish and mammals, where our intelligence changes through harmonizing and balancing our inner self through being permanently connected to the Collective Consciousness. It is up here where, through the mathematics, we learn to multiply and divide, not just add and subtract, and we can see through both our masculine and feminine thoughts. This is how the oceanic species are able to control their population through having the ability to change their sex. From the oceanic, we enter up into the base of the brain, where we must begin to learn all over again how to enter into the unconsciousness recognition of self. The ego refers to this area as the "heavenly realms". It is up here where we have entered into the world of the insect population; where everything is created through the sound waves of pure thought. Not a bad apartment to search for, is it?

The cat species represents "detachment", so, if a cat crosses your path, you are being reminded of your detachment from self. You are pulling yourself away from your own understanding. Come back home into self. These things can be presented to us at any time, so be aware of what the Collective Consciousness is reflecting back to your Higher Self in regard your thinking in that moment.

Stop for a moment and think these two words: "thank you" – your thinking those words not only changes the molecular structure of your self, it also commits your thoughts to the rest of the structure of the Collective Consciousness. Believe me, you are making a profound statement to every human. Take the chance to exalt your thinking, and then you can always be in the right place at the right time. Those happenings are all answering your thoughts. Your body is your supreme being. We are called "Hu-mans", as in "being human".

You can use the Sacred Alphabet and Sacred Numerology whilst you are sitting in your car in traffic. Decode the number plates of the cars around you; those signs are in your vision world for a reason – or, as some of you refer to it, a "coincidence". Now say that word correctly, breaking it up into syllables: "co-inside-essence", which is interpreting the "corporation inside the essence". Now we will reverse those words: "the essence inside the corporation". Interesting, isn't it, that this is the language of the brain, and what we refer to as the unconscious mind is also the energy of our Soul?

The letters and numbers on the cars coming towards you are the incoming messages regarding your day ahead. The ones going away from you are in regard to your thinking and where it is leading you in that moment. When I was heading off to work at my clinic for the day, I was always alerted to what my day could perceive for me through reading the numbers and letters around me as I travelled to work. I always read the number plates of the first seven vehicles; if it was a truck, it imparted a different message. (All these explanations are in other sections of the book concerning the subject.) In the beginning of my training, on a conscious level, I was innocently unaware of what I was doing; however, my subconscious mind was alerting me to the fact that my unconscious mind was directing back to me. I became more aware of the power of numbers. "How could this be so?" Was my cry to the Universe. "Why is everything so exact? How could this vision give me my immediate answers to all of my thoughts, so intellectually?" I became so excited when this information began to filter through my mind. Each time you see a car number plate, street, or city name, put the meanings of the Sacred Alphabet and Numerology together.

Here is an example of a number plate and its meaning:
MUW-9496. The letters M-U-W mean, "the mastering of my thought is through understanding my wisdom".

9 means: "Knowing all."

4 means: "My temple."

9 again: "Through my relationship of self, I know it all." In other words, you are allowed no excuses.

6 means: "Become the master of self."

Or we can read the message as the numbers 94 and 96. The number 94 it means, "through knowing all, I am my temple". The number 96 means, "through knowing all, I master my thoughts". That number plate is acknowledging that the principle thought that collected itself is available for you so that you can use the energy that unconsciously has been collected just for you. And this is the power of the mathematics of the mind; it is available for every human being, all at the same time.

CHAPTER TWENTY NINE

The Divine Language

As I have stated many times before, through the stories of the myth, the mind of the first time was the God "EL", whose mythical stories were brought forth through the intelligence of the Aryan kingdoms. "EL" – or Everlasting Life – was the Supreme Being, and the lesser Gods followed suit. Those Gods were other personalities of self who began to wake up; and then they began to mimic and follow in the steps of the first God. All this was through each one of our personalities inheriting and accepting the same story that we were able to create the next advanced thought, which woke up and became each cell's Collective Inheritance.

The light of these cells then collected other personalities that stood up to their own thoughts, and others followed suit. All of which is explaining to us the nomes of Egypt. The God "EL" represents the urging of our sexuality waking itself up. He became the Chief Executive of the Governmental Body. He empowered us to move forward as we journey up towards the second dimensional mind, which is the God "AN". Can you now understand how the word "pagan", which so many of you dismiss as idolatry, came into our dictionary? The word "pagan", when decoded, interprets as the "pages of 'AN'", which is the beginning of our Divine revelation of the pages of our educational intelligence unfolding itself – and which, for many of us, the ego still does not wish to define.

Through these ancient nomes – or Cities of Light – we begin to realize that, through the Asiatic languages, they are also referred to as the hidden chakras of the body. During my earlier training in Chinese medicine, I was taught that there were twenty-two chakras in the lower section of the body, and twenty in the upper section. Thank God for that lesson over thirty years ago! The information helped to set my mathematics in motion for my next education in understanding more of the Egyptian philosophies. Now remember that, through the Egyptian principles, this lower section of the body represents the Upper Kingdom of Egypt. The "upper kingdom" is our lower section of the body. Why? All the information that has been scribed throughout the Egyptian philosophies has been delivered to us intellectually from the unconscious mind; therefore, it is mirrored back to us.

Please remember that this is an introduction into the Divine language. There were supposedly twenty-one fields of light, which are represented in the upper section of the body (Lower Kingdom of Egypt), where the inner dictionary begins to transform through the experience of opening the heart to allow the angelic realms to be free. Do you remember the hieroglyph of Thoth weighing both the heart and the feather on the set of scales, and balancing them? So I began to put the story together, in relationship to the philosophies of Egypt and China, in order to understand the origin of the internal languages of the unconscious mind (as both of these countries have already earned their entry into the Divine language).

I strongly believe that Π (pi) has something to do with all these wisdoms coming together for us to be able to release our thoughts up into our sonic sound. I know that we can accomplish "pi" through the journey of discovering self, through attaining our complete hierarchical intelligence. It is a state of mind where there is no interference from any other glyph of thought. It is a state of complete enlightenment.

I am still trying to bring together the $3 \times 7 = 21$ – or is it the $7 \times 3 = 21$ – nomes of the Lower Kingdom. When I decode three times seven, it is informing me that my mind is my teacher, which is my light and the ultimate of my intellect. Therefore, my responsibility is placed under the auspicious command of my ego – or the left hemisphere of the brain. And, when I reverse the numbers to seven times three, it is informing me that my intellect is my light, and my light is my teacher, which is my mind; all this information is free to reverberate through the eternal pathways of my right brain. I have a strong belief that somewhere in amongst all these riddles, all is all connected to the symbolism of the seven seals in the Book of Revelations, which are the symbolic instructions informing us that the number seven is the inner teacher, through the culmination of our intuition serving us; all becomes available to us, once we have understood how we open up into the higher realms of the unconscious recognition of self.

Allow me to go on further with the explanations to the nomes of Egypt. How did we get the name "gnome" for our little people? Are they referred to as "God's nome" ("G-nome"), which means "God's gathering of intensified light"?

We have been informed of the twenty-two nomes – or counties – that come up the Nile from Abu Sanbel (traditionally, Abu Simbel), to what is known as Upper Egypt, and onward through to the old city of Memphis, or so the story is told. Now we know that, in relation to the human body, this area finishes up above the heart. Through the sacred language, this area is where we leave the past in order to apply ourselves to earning the Divine language of our inner self. Supposedly, the next area begins from above the heart, reverberating through the thymus area to collect another twenty-one nomes, which instigate our intelligence to enter up into the base of the brain. These nomes continue up through Cairo to Alexandria – or "EL-Ex-AN-Dri-EA", the crown of the head – which we now understand is the home of God. These are known as the Lower Kingdoms, where we bring our Divinity – or truth – together. All this information explains to you the Metaphysical resonance as to why both the Upper and Lower Kingdoms are reversed back down to us. Remember that the language was originally written and released back to us from the unconscious mind; not our conscious or subconscious three-dimensional minds. This is the home of the Gods, the Prophets, and the Sages!

We are now aware of the numbers of three (3) cycles of seven (7), which equals twenty-one (21). This story is also explaining to us the relationship we earn regarding the seven seals;' that is, as to how the animals were collected for the Ark, as told in the Old Testament, where Noah was asked by God to collect the clean beasts times seven. The code is explaining that we need one clean beast to fortify each one of these seals. I am explaining the plagues in the Book of Revelations, which represent those old irritations and insecurities of our mind that we have veiled around our self to protect it. I am explaining to you how we open our intelligence up into these seven seals in order to earn our crown; this explanation is equivalent to earning pi through human consciousness. Seven (7) seals, times three (3) – which is the third-dimensional Mind of God – equals twenty-one (21).

Let us go back over these words. In the first time, which is known metaphysically as the stories of the Old Testament, these villages – or nomes – were recorded to us as "Cities of Light", as to how the people moved towards them to feel that they were coming home. They became small states or districts where the people collected and found their contentment with self and one another – or so the original story goes. Each district supposedly represented a certain type of person who wanted to specialize in certain trades and practices.

My teachers in Egypt explained the story to me this way: If you had a yearning to learn a trade, you went to live in a certain area to begin your training. And while you lived there, you would learn to become specialized in your field of expertise. And, when each of the nomes began prospering, they had a complete formula for every human to be able to receive his/her ultimate benefit. All people had to do was to sail up or down the Nile to call in to other districts in order to receive what they needed to accomplish. This is still happening in many areas throughout Europe today, where you go to a certain village to buy your goods; they were originally called kingdoms. Are you seeing the symbolism in regard to the importance of the spinal column, which is the beginning of the human brain? Are these "Cities of Light" in the same area as the chakras in the body, as explained through Asian medicine?

How does all this information tie in with the Temple of Karnak ("Kha-AN-Ark", the "inner knowledge of 'AN', becoming your Ark") and the stroll down through the avenue to the Temple of Luxor. The avenue is supported with sphinxes on either side, which have been placed where they are representing our personalities – or thoughts – that have reached a level of their own attainment. Remember, we understand that, in the ancient times, the High Priests walked along this avenue with the Bja'Ark carried on their shoulders, answering the people calling out their questions, from where they gathered on either side of the avenue. If the High Priests had a positive answer, they stepped forward; if their answer was negative, they stepped backwards. Not one word was uttered by these priests. The callers had to go away and earn their own query regarding the symbolism that they were given. I am explaining many of the hieroglyphs that have been painted on the walls, where there were people supporting the ark. They are releasing to us the truth of the inner story. As we open up our intellect, we are strengthened by our self. We are replacing the missing links to teach our ego to reach up to achieve its highest level of attainment.

Remember, the design of the Sphinx is metaphysically representing your ego, which can only support itself through reminding you of your past. It is remembering where it came from, through trying to control you and lead you back into the primal mind. It represents the missing link that you must accomplish through accepting your self. Otherwise, we would all become repetitious performances of our parents!

My thought is that it is not representing a lion. My theory is that it is explaining the missing link between our past and our future. The statue of this animal is representing the God Anubis, the ancient loyalty of self – or the gatekeeper to the underworld or netherworld, where we learn to earn our freedom in order to be delivered up into the heavenly realms.

Anubis was automatically beheaded, once he had entered up into the ethereal realms of the unconscious mind, where the head of man was placed over his own! Otherwise, there would be no progress to create a future for any of us to endure. That is why the Sphinx is placed on the left-hand side of the Pyramids, to remind us of how we have evolved through unravelling our inner education so that we can become free of the restrictions of the past!

The metaphorical stories foretold in the ancient kingdoms are informing us that the Sphinx was previously known as the God Harmarchiiss; through the codes, this denotes as "Ha-Rha-Mha-Chi-Iss", and it explains to us how we "heavenly ascend to release the restrictions of our mind; through mastering self"; all through the relationship we earn from our mathematical intelligence that is embedded throughout these seven seals. I also believe that originally there was a moat that surrounded the Sphinx where the water was pumped in from the Nile which represented the ocean of consciousness. If you look at the body today you can see how the water marks are moving up the animal not eroding from above. This figure of the Sphinx was informing the people that while they had the bodily mind of the animal, the consciousness was always there to protect them.

There is a story that informs us of Tutmose, who became a Pharaoh. He supposedly replaced Hatshepsut, who reigned for the three cycles of seven, as the first female Pharaoh. Her temple is created in the Valley of the Kings, in the northern monastic area. It is constructed in a grand design that has three layered terraces of steps, which provide an entry into her temple. Tutmose is also supposed to be the father of Hatshepsut, so where do we go from here?

Through the Metaphysical resonance, we become aware, that we think it is Tutmose I who was her father; she inherited his land, and through her gestation of twenty-one years, each of the three Gods had birthed themselves seven times through the genetic relationship to her seven seals; hence, the three terraces which introduce us to the entrance of her temple! On the first and second terraces, where the statues once stood, we note that there are twenty-four doorways, twelve either side of the staircase, representing the twelve Gods of light and the twelve Gods of darkness being brought together – which explains the double helix of our DNA (twenty-four strands).

Hatshepsut had ascended up into the hierarchical mind, where her cast was rated to become a Pharaoh. How did we reach this decision? The crown she wore was a vulture with its wings spread over her head in the form of protection. Shamanically, we understand that the vulture is the one species that waits until the Soul has left the body before it devours the flesh! Therefore, she had ascended into the unconscious mind. Tutmose II followed in her footsteps, as he had previously birthed the feminine right brain in order to become harmonized and balanced.

The story continues to inform us that Tutmose stood before the Sphinx, which was buried up to its neck in the sand. He received a vision, where the Sphinx explained to him that, if he would free him self of his bondage and clear away the sand, he could then complete his task and would become a Pharaoh – the heir to his own throne. By now, through your Metaphysical education, you can understand that this story is explaining to you that, if you clear away the past, the future is revealed to you – and that is where you inherit your own throne.

Is this what these old royal decrees were explaining to us? Are those nomes the introduction and connection to the Hermetic Codes? Does our information collects in certain areas, just as the ancient Egyptians collected their information to educate themselves? Let me say this word again, through the codes: "He-Rah-Met-Ic". This word is similar to the word "Hermes", who was the messenger of the Gods, and who is here to show us the way to achieve the royal mathematics of our mind. Remember that the Avenue of Sphinxes represents our personalities that have earned their truth and are silently supporting us, until we can believe more in ourselves.

I like to think of them as my support team, where, as an Apprentice, I am learning to master myself – to become an Adept. The Avenue of Sphinxes played a major part in my vision world twenty years ago as I was earning all of this information. I watched as one of my personalities earned its place and changed into a sphinx to salute me; that was how I understood the information back then.

To release these codes, I had to work long and hard during this excursion in order to find the answers to these symbolic wings of Ma'at – which is also referred to as the Bodhisattva energy, as explained through the Asiatic principles. We see the continuing journey of the first God "EL" discovering his own intelligence through releasing his fears – or plagues – in order to ascend up into his royal acclaim. These nomes of Egypt, are the doorways into the sacred initiations that must be accepted by the ego, where it learns to become a Divine principle to serve the emotional mind, which can only be achieved through its understanding itself. Through the codes of the Sacred Numerology, the number twenty-two (22) is revealed as the Power of the Magician. It is where the relationship of both left and right brain must view each other equally; it all depends on how they share the responsibility to accept the communication of the mind in the moment.

The mathematical conversion to "pi" is 22/7. I want to go slowly here in order for you to see and hear how I repeat this to you. Through the decrees of the Lower Kingdom, there was once a High Priest called Shemag who was in charge of these twenty-two (22) nomes. The word "Shemag" – or "Chi-magi", as it is pronounced in Arabic – denotes as, "the energy of the magician". Throughout my Shamanic training, I was taught to understand this power that mathematically collects when the personalities of the mind are measured and balanced, which allows the magician to have the choice of using both hemispheres of the brain as a oneness. He can walk with the light or the dark; it is all up to the pituitary gland as to the emotional responses that are released through the proprietary attitude of thought.

Might I add here that, in the German language, the word "magician" is interpreted as "Magie", and this word leads on to symbolizing the meaning of the word "major", which became "mayor" in the English language; he holds the majority voice of his party and symbolically represents the citizens that abide in his city. The word "major" is also a titled commission earned in the armed forces, and such an officer is responsible for his troops.

Do you think that these twenty-two (22) nomes could be our understanding, and the other twenty-one (21), our action? Or could this explanation be twenty-one (21) in the Lower kingdom – plus, the I AM – and twenty-two (22) in the Upper kingdom? Why does my statue have twenty-two (22) arms on the left side and twenty-two (22) arms on the right? Remember that this is in tune with the opening of the heart that is presented to us through the hieroglyph of Thoth holding the scales with the heart on one side and the feather on the other, in perfect balance. Is this number "pi" (22/7) related to the magician earning and opening up the seven (7) seals – or what the Arabic and Asian languages refer to as the seven (7) harmonies? Is this how "pi" – or "PHI" – is collaborated through the opening of the heart? We are all here to understand how to reach the Oracle in order to act on behalf of our Divine intelligence.

I can now begin to understand how the mathematics begins to exalt this number of 22/7 into empowering us up into the next resonance of our nation. I also understand now that the three Pyramids north of Cairo are the temple structure of the three Gods, which are situated at the base of the brain. Please believe me when I say to you that, in order to bring all this information together, my confusion reigned supreme.

The Chinese language – or their belief – is also created in the Summer Palace, the huge, imposing octahedral tower, which is three stories high and also has four layers of eaves. Please refer back to the numerical codes to decode that the house of the statue of the Bodhisattva is representing the three minds of God, reaching up to the temple mind. The statue is 36.44 metres high (please decode again) of the Guanshiyin Buddha, who represents the emotional responses pertaining to the Bodhisattva energy.

They also have the belief that the God/Goddess, (balanced mind or Akhenaton) Guan Ean – or, as it is pronounced through the English language, "Quanyin" – symbolically represents the two brains as yin and yang. (Or is it yang and yin? They all mean exactly the same thing! It is just that one steps before the other.)

The statue that I have in front of me as I write these words was given to me as a gift from my students in Asia, and it originally came from a temple in Tibet that was demolished during a mudslide. It has five layers of eleven heads; three heads on three layers, one larger head on those, and a new born baby on the fifth layer. Two feathers come up from behind these last two heads, which represent the crown of Ma'at (as explained in the Egyptian philosophies). There are twenty-two (22) arms on the right side and twenty-two (22) arms on the left (this is the statue I referred to earlier). The hand of each arm has a gift carved into it. These symbolically represent our wings in flight through the angelic realms; and, in each hand, are the tools that we can call upon and use: scrolls, knives, balls of string, mirrors, axes, flames, seals, pearls, rings, etc. So these eleven heads are announcing to us their interpretation of the strands of their DNA unfolding themselves. They are here to support us through every thought we think. Please remember, through everything you have read before, that you now understand that the angelic realm is the house of Ma'at – or the house of the mathematics of the mind – which defines the Divine mathematics of our mind, once we have opened our heart to our self! The arms symbolically represent the wings, through releasing the flight of the mind – or her symbol through the Egyptian philosophies. Remember, Metaphysics is looking through, not at; and it can only be attained through discovering self!

I remember watching my children unfold their intelligence when they were young. I could see how they were using my intellect, which I had passed on to them, in order to get them to release their own intellect. I always wore an apron when I was in the house. My apron came in very handy for me to wipe my hands, protect me from my spills in the kitchen, and wipe the occasional fork or spoon to clean it to be reused in the moment! Imagine my surprise as I watched my daughter one morning automatically reach out with a spoon in her left hand to wipe it down the left hand side of her dress. I always used my right hand, and she automatically reached for her left. Before I could chastise her, I had to think out this deliberate move on her part, in my mind. If I used my right hand, then why did she use her left hand? What responsibility of her inheritance had to release for her to use the same idea? Is this the foundation of how our ego collects itself? Even to this day, when I visit my children, I hear my sons telling their children, "Does that object have 'toy' written on it?" "No, dad," they say. "Then why are you playing with it?" Oh, shades of the parent's mind!

Can you now understand and see how we can achieve the vibration of "pi"? As our intelligence collects, ultimately reaching up to open the hymen on top of our pineal gland, our intellect is royally seated in the house of God. This answers the myth where we become the lighthouse from Alexandria that is seen from the four corners of the earth, becoming humanity's ultimate aim, where we can live in the library of our mind.

We have much more affirmation now to understand why the ancient ones, right through to the early biblical artists, painted the crown of the head with a circle of light. That light represents the light acclaimed through the earnings of the Mind of God, and it also reminds us of the stories of the tallest lighthouse in Alexandria, whose beam was seen from the four corners of the earth. This is our freedom. Read the Book of Daniel, chapter 2, for further confirmation.

These pages are only a brief introduction to the Sacred Codes. I do not apologize for the amount of repeated references that you read over and over again throughout the books in this volume, as they give you an added opportunity to allow this new thinking to search and find new wealth to create an expansion into your intelligence. Once it becomes repetitious, it allows you to opens up into the next dimension of your mind.

All is revealed when you can hear your thoughts, not just listen to them. Through just listening, you will find that your life will repeat the same experiences over and over again. Can you see how you are creating your own hologram? Each new facet creates its own shining light, through the confidence you release by harmonizing and balancing yourself.

Oh, my goodness, here it is! These are the final paragraphs for me to write regarding the information you need to understand the Sacred Alphabet and Numerology. These are my tutorials; they will take time to reopen in you, just as it has taken many years and millions of my spoken words to rescribe this ancient language into a language that, one day, you will accept regarding your heavenly realms. It is still alive and living in every one of us; my aim is to bring it back into a compatible resonance that I hope you can understand as to how the stories of Egypt were originally scribed on the walls. They are all explaining the language you have inherited through your genes! I could go on and on describing the oneness of humanity's intelligence. Open the window of your mind.

This book has been the greatest temptation that has been placed before me. May you enjoy your walk, through discovering your internal nesting place! I have not touched on the Egyptian Book of the Dead; to explain the inner language of those codes would take another million words to write. Suffice it to say that these books are explaining how you commit your thoughts in order to collect your wisdom and speak your truth. These are the myths that have been brought forth and placed in the Holy Bible, which we are still reading today.

There is brilliance out there from people who believe in themselves. Their light keeps you alive! Bring the science of religion – or the religion of science – together, just as God and the Laws of the Universe began with! Remember that they are both equal, and both represent the left and right hemispheres of your brain. These stories are all about you and your capabilities and accomplishments. It is up to you to realign yourself! Finally, please pour yourself a nice big glass of water, drink it slowly, and thank yourself every time you swallow – as that water turns into the wine, or the nectar from the Gods, it will heal me!

Thank you for reading my story.

Books By O.M. Kelly (Omni)

Decoding The Mind Of God

Author O.M. Kelly's seminal work, "Decoding the Mind of God", is a compilation of nine volumes of metaphysical information based on the research into the coded information of the Laws of the Universe, also known as the Collective Consciousness, and represents a groundbreaking contribution to our understanding of the metaphysical universe. Now, all nine volumes are being released as separate, revised books, each offering a unique perspective on the universe's workings. Omni's work has been widely acclaimed for its depth of insight, and her contributions to the field of metaphysics have been groundbreaking.

The nine separate volumes encompassing:

The Laws of the Universe
Thought
Dis-Ease
Death
Sexuality and Spirituality
The Dolphin's Breath
Sacred Alphabet and Numerology
Sacred Fung Shwa
Extra-Terrestrial Intelligence.

Updated version of each book now being released separately.

Book I. Decoding The Laws Of The Universe

If you're looking to unlock the hidden potential within you and transform your life, "Decoding the Laws of the Universe" is the book for you. This powerful and insightful book is designed to help you understand the deeper, metaphysical aspects of life and tap into the transformative power of the universe utilising the secrets of our Individual Universal Law.

This book serves to introduce you into the secrets of our Individual Universal Law. This amazing knowledge and wisdom, is transformative on a personal level and creates the opportunity for you to interrelate with the Laws of the Universe. Throughout this book, you will dive deep into the inner workings of your mind and discover the hidden laws that govern your life. You will learn about the alchemy of the mind and how to harness its power to create positive change in your life and the world around you. Through the lens of Metaphysical philosophy, you will gain a new perspective on the world and your place in it. You will learn how the universe communicates with you through coded intelligence and how to unlock the hidden messages that are all around you.

This book is a journey for personal transformation and spiritual growth. Take a voyage of exploration of the expansive vistas of information discovering the codes of Metaphysics and the Quest of Life. You will learn the Metaphysical coded wisdom of the ancients for the necessary mind elements to transit into a higher mindset. Explore the secret relationship between the Earth and human beings, the higher mind, the Metaphysical journey, the importance of self, belief in self, the codes of mythology, a higher level of attainment, releasing the past, fears and evolving one's light on a Metaphysical level, what causes stress, work place promotion and why it does not happen, and many other topics. Included is a short overview of the conventional Twelve Laws of the Universe.

Book II. Decoding Thought
Welcome to a journey of self-discovery and exploration of the mysteries of the universe. "Decoding Thought" is a ground-breaking book that explores the power of the mind and the principles of metaphysical thought. Through a deep exploration of the mind and body connection, the author provides readers with insights to unlock the full potential of their thoughts. This book provides a guide to harnessing the power of the mind to create the life you desire. With explanations of metaphysical principles, the book makes these often complex concepts accessible to readers. "Decoding Thought" takes you on a journey through the vast landscape of the human mind. Explore the mysteries of thought power, and how it can shape our reality and transform our lives. The power of thought is not just a theoretical concept. It is a tangible force that can be harnessed to bring about significant changes in our lives.

This book can expand your consciousness and open your mind to new possibilities. By exploring the metaphysical principles that underlie our existence, you can gain a new perspective on life and the world around you. This book provides through a metaphysical interpretation explanations into the various aspects of thought power, including how it is linked to our DNA, and the roles played by the pituitary and pineal glands in our thought processes. O.M. Kelly also explains the metaphysical language in reference to the codes of the Egyptian Philosophies, the Bible, myths, cultures, and how they connect to the power of thought. The journey continues with a deep dive into the inner Secret School of Metaphysics, where we discover the Alchemy of the Brain and the pathway to our truth. Discover the unconscious/higher mind, and our Life Quest, which opens the doors to the Psychometric Consciousness. Through the lens of metaphysical interpretation, you will gain a new perspective on the impact of thought on our mental and emotional states that includes a look at Depression, Coping with Change and how to retrain our brain patterns to be positive and moving forward for our Financial Abundance and manifesting prosperity. The book ends with a brief overview of the brain/mind, and a short Q&A on thought power. This metaphysical book on the power of thought is a guide to discovering your true potential and creating the life you desire.

"Decoding Thought" is a must-read for anyone seeking to unlock the full potential of their mind and harness the power of the universe to create a life of fulfilment and this book serves as an invaluable resource.

Book III. Decoding Dis-Ease

Introducing "Decoding Dis-Ease" a Metaphysical Interpretation into understanding the intricate web of factors that contribute to our health and well-being. From the author of several groundbreaking works on the interaction of the mind and body, this book delves into a wide range of topics related to dis-ease. It is a fascinating and insightful book that offers a fresh perspective on health and healing. It is a must-read for anyone interested in the mind-body connection.

Readers will be inspired to embark on a quest of discovering the codes within themselves, recognizing that every cell in our body is pure Cosmic Consciousness. They will also gain a deeper understanding of specific health topics such as the thyroid, the kidneys, men's problems, and many other topics from a Metaphysical perspective. The book also examines how a dis-ease is given to us in group energy and the complex interplay between our bodies and minds, and how every human has the consequences of all that we do and experience.

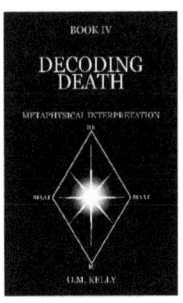

Book IV. Decoding Death

Looking for a thought-provoking exploration of death and the afterlife? Look no further than O.M. Kelly's book, "Decoding Death".

"Decoding Death takes us on a transformative Metaphysical journey through the mysteries of the Universe. O.M. Kelly—known as Omni—provides an expanded horizon of possibilities, awareness, and a transformative perspective. In this book, Omni delves into a wide range of topics related to dying and death, from the loss of a loved one to a viewing of the afterlife. Omni has a unique ability to view the Laws of the Universe using her extraordinary state of heightened awareness and multi-dimensional perception and through the lens of metaphysics offers a unique perspective on the nature of death and what it means for the human experience.

Omni shares personal experiences and stories, including the passing of her late husband, brother, and parents, and offers a metaphysical insight for those dealing with loss and grief. She explores the transformational process of death and the potential for spiritual growth and enlightenment. The book explains that the human experience of death is part of a larger Universal process that is ultimately guided by a higher intelligence referred to as God (Laws of the Universe/Collective Consciousness) or whatever name you prefer. Omni's exploration of death is both metaphysically comprehensive and thought-provoking, offering readers a deep and nuanced understanding of one of life's greatest mysteries. With chapters on the Three Doorways—Three Stages of Death, The Quantum Hologram—Why a partner dies for the other partner to progress in the "Journey of Life", The Passing to the Afterlife, and many other enlightening chapters, "Decoding Death" offers a unique viewpoint. By drawing on a range of religious, philosophical, and metaphysical perspectives, Omni offers a compelling vision of the human experience of death and its role in the larger Universal Law.

Book V. Decoding Sexuality And Spirituality

Welcome to "Decoding Sexuality and Spirituality" by O.M. Kelly. In this book, explore the fascinating relationship between our sexuality and spirituality, and how these two aspects of ourselves are intimately intertwined. Delve into the concept that sexuality is the doorway to our spirituality, and examine the powerful and transformative energy that is generated when we fully embrace our sexual selves. The book also explores the notion of the metaphysical orgasmic cloud, and how it can be used to deepen our connection to our spiritual selves. We will also examine the role of marriage in our sexual and spiritual lives.

For women, the book offers a unique perspective on the journey of embracing sexuality and spirituality, as well as insights into the different stages of life and how they impact our sexual and spiritual selves. Drawing on both ancient wisdom traditions and metaphysical mythology, the book examines the myth of Hercules and how it relates to our sexual intelligence. By decoding the symbolism of this myth, we can gain a deeper understanding of the ways in which our sexuality and spirituality intersect and influence each other. So if you are ready to embark on a journey of self-discovery and unlock the true potential of your sexual and spiritual selves, then "Decoding Sexuality and Spirituality" is the book for you.

VI. Decoding The Dolphin's Breath

"Decoding The Dolphin's Breath" by O.M. Kelly (Omni) is a captivating exploration of the relationship between humans and dolphins. The book begins with a poignant account of a real-life encounter between the author and a group of wild dolphins, setting the stage for a deep dive into the spiritual and metaphysical significance of dolphins. This captivating book takes readers on a journey into the heart of the dolphin-human relationship, exploring the ways in which these majestic creatures can help us attune to the power of free will, and telepathic communication.

Throughout the Laws of Shamanism the wonderful Dolphin in consciousness, represents the attainment we can reach through ourselves earning our freedom of will. This book explains the benefits of the dolphins breath—the why and how we use the breath that influences our divine mentality. Further, it's a story which reveals how the dolphins have taught us the process to be free of fear, and to tap into the Language of Babylon—to understand the language of Earth. One of the key themes of the book is the idea that dolphins are always breathing their total freedom of thought, and the author provides insights into how humans can learn from this remarkable trait. The book also invites readers to embark on a journey into understanding the telepathic communication of whales and dolphins. Inclusive in the book is a written meditation which assists you to connect to the external consciousness and release the fear that you have wrapped around yourself for protection.

Overall, this book offers a unique and fascinating perspective on the metaphysics of dolphins, and will appeal to anyone interested in spirituality, and the power of the mind.

Book VII. Decoding The Sacred Alphabet And Numerology

This book offers a myriad of explanations concerning the higher consciousness in relationship to names, places and numbers. "Decoding The Sacred Alphabet & Numerology" by O.M. Kelly (Omni) is a thought-provoking and enlightening read that

offers a unique perspective on the metaphysical world of letters and numbers.

Omni's insights and teachings are sure to inspire readers to deepen their understanding of the ancient sacred codes to names of places, your name and the sacred alphabet. The author also delves into the practice of metaphysical numerology, which involves using numerical values to interpret personality traits, life paths, and other aspects of a person's life. Omni explains how metaphysical numerology can be used to gain insight into our spiritual path and to better understand our purpose in life. Your ability to decipher the Sacred Alphabet and Numerology codes commonly and constantly presented to you throughout your life, will open opportunities to expand your consciousness and awareness you never thought possible.

Embark on a journey through the myth of Babylon and Shambhala and discover the sacred language that connects us all. Explore Luxor, the Delta Giza Saqqara and Faiyum, and Solomon's Temple, and uncover the mysteries of Akhenaton and Tomb KV-63. Find out how to unravel the threads of your DNA and unlock the ancient knowledge of the Old Aramaic Story of Aladdin and the Lamp. Explore Grecian stories through the Metaphysical language and travel along the Old Silk Road. Discover the Shamanic inheritance of numbers and their meanings, and learn how we rely on numbers to read the hidden language of the universe. Join O.M. Kelly on a journey of self-discovery and uncover the divine language within.

Book VIII. Decoding Sacred Fung Shwa

Introducing "Decoding Sacred Fung Shwa", the revolutionary guide to understanding and harnessing the energy within your home and yourself. In this book, author O.M. Kelly (Omni), has introduced a metaphysical sixth element that takes our understanding of energy to the next level. By incorporating "Your Life Force," we gain deeper insight into the connection between our homes and our emotional well-being. Discover the power of Fung Shwa and learn how to use it to create a balanced and harmonized environment that supports your mind, body, and Soul.

The book explains the meaning of Sacred Fung Shwa to the Shamanistic principles that underpin it. Delve into the metaphysical medicine wheel and explore the elements of life, before moving on to practical applications of Fung Shwa in the home.

Learn how to visualize your home as a collective energy and clear the clutter to enhance its flow. Discover your Astrological colours and how they can be used in Fung Shwa design, from the kitchen to the bedroom and beyond. Explore the compatibility of personal colours in relationships, and discover the power of paintings, pictures, and mirrors to enhance your home's energy.

But Fung Shwa isn't just about the home—we also explore its applications in the office environment and in small retail businesses. Learn how to apply Fung Shwa principles to a clothing store, shoe store, or café, even discover the role of Fung Shwa in money, and to Metaphysical Numerology.

Throughout it all, we focus on the quest of life and how Fung Shwa can help you achieve your goals and live your best life. So what are you waiting for? Dive into the world of Fung Shwa and transform your home, your business, and your life today!

Book IX. Decoding Extra-Terrestrial Intelligence

Are you ready to embark on a journey of self-discovery? Look no further than O.M. Kelly's groundbreaking book, Book IX "Decoding Extra-Terrestrial Intelligence". Through metaphysical interpretation, O.M. Kelly (Omni) has unlocked the secrets of the universe and revealed that the key to our next step in human evolution lies within ourselves. This book will show you how to tap into the indelible imprint of holographic importance that is seeded within every human, and unleash the Extra-Terrestrial Intelligence that resides within you. Omni shares her own personal journey of encountering Beings of Light and how it has transformed her understanding of the universe and humanity's place within it.

Omni presents the concept that we all have Extra-Terrestrial Intelligence, and have the ability to tap into the vast knowledge and secrets of the universe. The ancient civilizations left behind clues and teachings about this metaphysical existence and it is up to us to continue to uncover and advance the way we think. Through this journey of life, we can unlock the secrets of our own consciousness and tap into the full potential of our existence. This is a fascinating exploration of the mysteries of the universe and the potential for our own personal evolution.

Readers who are interested in self-transformation through universal truths, Metaphysical exploration for personal growth and a journey of self-discovery would be interested in reading this insightful book on contact with Beings of Light and Extra-terrestrial Intelligence, exploring ancient civilizations and the knowledge they possessed about the universe and the human mind.

Power Thought for the Day Oracle Book

"Power Thought For The Day Oracle Book" provides insights to assist you on your life path. Through the "Totem" energy of all, the ancient species that have evolved before us, represent an emotional inheritance that we can rely on to sustain the moment. Each species that has evolved on this planet is recorded into our cellular memory. This book with 22 Major Arcana Shamanic Power Animal Totems provides a contemporary metaphysical interpretation symbolic of our evolution. By selecting a page of the book the Shamanic animal will provide an insight in how you are thinking at this moment in time. Through the contemporary Laws of Shamanism (with a metaphysical interpretation), O.M. Kelly (Omni) has produced a book that will assist the "Path of the Initiate" in emotional intelligence when our mind is in the field of doubt. When we become aware of how we are thinking it is a catalyst for transformation. This compact little book is a handy 4 x 7 inches or 10.2 x 17.8 cm to fit into your pocket or handbag.

How to use the book:
Our higher mind has no time; it steps into and works on behalf of the thought of the moment. This book encompasses 22 Major Totem Power representations, symbolic of our evolution. Close your eyes and inhale and exhale a deep breath and relax and allow yourself no thought as you select the right page of the Shamanic animal presented in this book. The right page will always appear for you at the right moment and you will discover how the power animals are working with you for insight into their wisdom. Different power animals come into our lives at various phases offering messages to guide us on our path.

Decoding the Shaman Within

In "Decoding the Shaman Within" international author O.M. Kelly (Omni) shares her Shamanic metaphysical journey. It would be termed a contemporary Shamanic initiation journey; a powerful spiritual enlightenment and transformational voyage of discovering the codes of Metaphysics and the Quest of Life. Through the sacred passage of time Omni discovered the secret codes of the Collective Consciousness (Laws of the Universe) to trek a higher level of consciousness. Throughout

Omni's training to receive the breath of Shamanism, many Elders from other cultures came to Australia and initiated her into their own tribal laws. Most of these Elders were men who arrived on Omni's doorstep uninvited but had received the call from the Universe to pass on their knowledge. Those magnificent people who had also earned their Shamanic experiences, only stayed long enough to give Omni their gift of consciousness and to initiate her into a new Shamanic name, which their tribe had bestowed, and then they disappeared out of Omni's life as quickly as they had come into it.

The Shamanic path in a Metaphysical perspective is the oldest pathway of the tribal law through the evolution of humanity. The Shaman is trained in the ancient language that is instilled in every genetic code that humanity carries within their DNA; you either have the opportunity to open it up and use it, or you just don't bother and choose to ignore it! It is as simple as that!

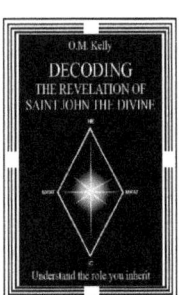

Decoding the Revelation of Saint John the Divine: Understand the role you inherit

The amazing breakthrough book "Decoding the Revelation of Saint John the Divine: Understand the role you inherit", is for anyone with an open, inquiring mind, seeking answers to the surreal descriptions of Earth's final days.

Through years of research O.M. Kelly interprets the cryptology behind the codes of mythology and various religions and has Metaphysically interpreted how the Holy Bible had been written through the original codex of Egyptology. The biblical stories were collected and condensed through the educated minds of that time.

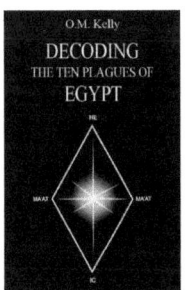

Decoding the Ten Plagues of Egypt

"Decoding the Ten Plagues of Egypt" presents a fresh insight into understanding the hidden structure of the language of how the Bible was written. The reader is introduced to the step by step Metaphysical decoding of the mystifying language, regarding the plagues from the Book of Exodus, Chapters: 7-12 in the Bible.

For the first time in contemporary history the essence of the Book of Exodus and its previously unsolved intriguing language will be revealed to provide deeper knowledge and clearer perception to unlock the significance the Book of Exodus is explaining to us.

Decoding Dreams

In "Decoding Dreams" international author O.M. Kelly (Omni), introduces a metaphysical interpretation of the dreams we dream. At times, we may believe that dreams allow us to peer into another world. O.M. Kelly provides the codes for us to understand that other world of dreams—or, through the Shamanic Principles, our "Vision Worlds". Dreams are created through your unconscious/higher mind communicating back to you; dreams are reminding you of the lessons that you need to understand regarding yourself. You cannot hear them if your mind is filled with incessant chatter. The ego refuses to conform when it is in control of the moment. Dreams can range from a pleasant dream, which could be a recommendation to add to what you are doing, to a nightmare, which is a wake-up call from your higher self regarding what you are doing to yourself. As you read this book, keep in mind that learning to metaphysically interpret your dreams is a step-by-step process. Areas covered in the book are: Dream Representations (Animal Kingdom and the Human Kingdom), Questions and Answers about Dreams, and Dream Interpretations.

Reprint coming in the near future.

Notes:

www.ingramcontent.com/pod-product-compliance
Lightning Source LLC
Chambersburg PA
CBHW051538010526
44107CB00064B/2772